The Civil War on the Lower Kansas-Missouri Border

LARRY WOOD

Third Edition

Hickory Press
Joplin, Missouri

Published by:
      Hickory Press
      Joplin, Missouri

ISBN: 978-0-9702829-7-2

Library of Congress Control Number: 2016910832

Table of Contents

List of Illustrations

Preface

The geographic limits for this book remain the same as they were for the first two editions. The lower Kansas-Missouri border is defined as that part of the common border south of the Cass-Bates county line in Missouri or the Linn-Miami county line in Kansas. The border area is defined as extending approximately fifty miles east into Missouri and fifty miles west into Kansas. The narrow geographic limits purposely exclude several notable episodes of the Civil War, such as Quantrill's raid on Lawrence and the Battle of Wilson's Creek, which occurred in the general area of the Kansas-Missouri border but have been well documented by previous authors.

No new chapters have been added to his edition, but nearly all of the existing chapters have seen minor changes or additions. Also, the appendix, listing current places of Civil War interest in the lower Kansas-Missouri area, has been updated, and a number of the photos used in this edition differ from the ones used previously.

LOWER KANSAS-MISSOURI BORDER AREA

Map of Lower Kansas-Missouri Border Area

1
Rehearsals for War and the Engagement at Carthage

In the 1860 presidential election, Republican Abraham Lincoln garnered only about ten percent of the vote in the slave-holding border state of Missouri, and Southern Democrat John C. Breckinridge received only about nineteen percent, while two centrist candidates divided the remaining seventy-one percent. During the late winter and early spring of 1861, after South Carolina and other Southern states had seceded from the Union, the three distinct political camps that arose in Missouri in regard to the question of secession generally reflected the outcome of this recent election.[1]

The Unconditional Unionists fully supported the Federal government's effort to bring the seceding states back into the Union. This party was led by Congressman Frank P. Blair, Jr. of St. Louis, where the state's large, fiercely Unionist German population was concentrated.

At the other end of the political spectrum, the secessionist faction favored immediately joining the Confederacy. Governor Claiborne Fox Jackson was the group's most prominent spokesman, and his secessionist sentiment dominated in some outlying, rural counties, especially in the western part of the state and along the Missouri and Mississippi rivers.

The largest group, however, were the Conditional Unionists. Although many in this centrist camp held Southern sympathies, their position of "armed neutrality" meant that they would support the Union as long as the Federal military did not try to reclaim the seceding states by force or to occupy the state of Missouri. General Sterling Price was a leader of this compromise group. A Mexican War veteran and an ex-governor of the state, Price headed a convention in St. Louis at which delegates voted almost unanimously on March 8 to remain in the Union.

After the bombardment of the Federal installation at Ft. Sumter by Confederate troops in South Carolina on April 12, 1861, however, the chances of compromise faded. Two days later President Lincoln called for 75,000 volunteers for service in the Union army, and Missouri was asked to furnish four regiments as its quota. Governor Jackson refused to comply, declaring that the state would not furnish one dollar or one man for the President's "unholy crusade."[2]

Instead, the governor got a resolution passed through the legislature condemning any attempt by the Federal government to coerce the seceding states. Jackson also began trying to organize state troops for defense of Missouri, and, although the legislature was not as quick to support this effort, on April 20 Confederate sympathizers in Jackson and Clay Counties seized the Federal arsenal at Liberty to provide arms for the state troops.

Meanwhile, Congressman Blair began recruiting men in the St. Louis area for the Federal government and secured a company of infantry under Captain Nathaniel Lyon to come to St. Louis from Fort Riley, Kansas, to help in the effort. Tapping the militant Union fever of a group called the Wide-Awakes that had been drilling in the area throughout the spring, Blair had soon enlisted ten regiments, who commenced drilling under Captain Lyon.

On the 10th of May a contingent of about 700 of Governor Jackson's state militiamen under General Daniel. M. Frost assembled for training at Camp Jackson in St. Louis a few miles from the Federal arsenal. Many of Frost's men had been drawn from a rabid secessionist group called the Minutemen, who, like their counterpart, had been training for weeks, and Lyon believed they meant to seize the arsenal, although Frost disavowed such an intention.

With several thousand Federal troops, Lyon captured and disarmed the militiamen at Camp Jackson and marched them as prisoners toward the arsenal. Angry, pro-Southern demonstrators gathered and pelted the Federal troops with rocks as they paraded the captives through the streets of St. Louis, and a drunken man reportedly fired a pistol shot at the Union soldiers. Some of Lyon's troops rashly opened fire on the crowd, and almost thirty civilians were killed in the melee, including two women and a child.

The action infuriated secessionists and conditional Unionists alike, and the Missouri legislature now quickly approved Governor Jackson's plans to raise a state military force. It was designated the Missouri State Guard, and on May 15 Governor Jackson appointed Sterling Price as commander with a rank of major general. Nine military districts were established in the state with a brigadier general commanding each district. James S. Rains, former state senator from Sarcoxie, was placed in charge of the 8th District, which encompassed all of the Missouri counties along the lower Kansas border.

In an attempt to keep the war out of Missouri, General Price met in St. Louis with General William S. Harney, Union Commander of the West, and reached an agreement that Price would maintain order in Missouri and that Federal troops would, in turn, not intervene in state affairs. Blair and Lyon, however, saw the accord as a ruse. They felt that Governor Jackson was merely trying to stall while he trained his troops and made arrangements to join forces with the Confederacy. Blair influenced President Lincoln to replace Harney with Captain Lyon, who was promoted to brigadier general.

Jackson and Price sought a conference with the new general in hopes of maintaining the terms of the Price-Harney Agreement. In a June 11th meeting at the Planter's Hotel in St. Louis, Jackson proposed to disband the Missouri State Guards and try to keep peace in the state if General Lyon would disband the Union's Missouri volunteers, but the zealous Lyon was not in a bargaining mood. He felt a Federal presence in Missouri was necessary to protect loyal citizens, and he declared that he would see everybody in Missouri dead before he would let the state dictate to the U.S. government. "This means war!" he told Jackson and Price, and he sent an envoy to escort them beyond the Union lines in St. Louis.[3]

Governor Jackson and General Price retreated to Jefferson City, burning bridges and cutting telegraph wires along the way to disrupt the Federal lines of transportation and communication. The governor issued a proclamation calling for fifty thousand volunteers to repel the Federal "invasion" and ordered the commanders of the State Guard to concentrate their men at Boonville and Lexington. Then he and other state officials abandoned the capital. Governor Jackson with a portion of the State Guard moved the seat of government to Boonville, while General Price and the remainder of the state troops encamped at Lexington.

Meanwhile, General Lyon dispatched three regiments to southwest Missouri to secure that region and to cut off a possible southern retreat by the state troops. Lyon himself started upriver from St. Louis by steamboat with the remainder of his force, about 2,000 men.

He disembarked at Jefferson City and occupied the deserted capital for the Union, then continued upriver to Boonville, where, on June 17, he caught up with Jackson and about 1,500 of his state troops, commanded by the governor's nephew, Colonel John S. Marmaduke. When the fighting commenced, the undisciplined and poorly armed state troops scattered so quickly in the face of the booming Federal cannons that the skirmish was afterwards dubbed the "Boonville Races."

Governor Jackson retreated south as Lyon took over Boonville, and the next day General Price abandoned Lexington and also started south. The governor required a safer place to establish his seat of government, and General Price needed time to train and equip the fledgling Missouri State Guard. Leaving General Rains in command of his troops, Price rode ahead with a cavalry escort to scout out the southwest corner of the state for a suitable location for these endeavors and to seek the support of General Ben McCulloch, whose Confederate army occupied northwest Arkansas. Meanwhile, the separate forces under Governor Jackson and General Rains marched south and reunited at Lamar, where recruits for the State Guard were being mustered.

Marching from St. Louis, the Union army reached Springfield on June 24 and secured the town for the Federals. Upon learning of the possible linking of Governor Jackson's Missouri State Guard with McCulloch's Confederate regulars, Colonel Franz Sigel, a veteran of the German insurrection of 1848, determined to cut off such a juncture. Sigel impressed some horses and wagons from citizens around Springfield and struck for Sarcoxie with his own Third Brigade of Missouri Volunteers, part of the Fifth Brigade, a company of regular U.S. troops, and an eight-piece artillery battery, but no cavalry. His command totaled about 1,100 men and was made up mostly of St. Louis Germans, whom citizens of southwest Missouri derisively called the "Yankee Dutch."

Colonel Sigel reached Sarcoxie on the 28th and learned that Price was camped south of Neosho and that Governor Jackson was at Lamar. Sigel sent one company to secure Neosho, although his first bit of intelligence proved obsolete, as Price had already left for Arkansas. With the rest of his force, the colonel started toward Carthage. Erroneously assuming that General Lyon was not far behind Jackson, Sigel planned to stall the governor's southern advance long enough to let General Lyon catch up and crush the state troops from the rear. Sigel camped on the evening of July 4 at a springs on the east edge of Carthage, forcing a small detachment of

Franz Sigel commanded the Union forces at Carthage. *Library of Congress.*

the State Guard, which had been detailed to the town as a foraging party, to fall back toward Lamar. Each side, though, was now aware of the other's presence in the vicinity, and a clash of arms was inevitable.

That same evening, Jackson and Rains, with the main body of state troops, were camped below Lamar about twenty miles to the north. Their forces now consisted of well over 5,000 men, including

11

about 3,500 mounted troops and approximately 2,000 infantry and artillerymen. About 2,000 of the cavalrymen bore no weapons at all but were riding south in hopes of acquiring them. Many of the rest of the horsemen were outfitted just with an old squirrel rifle, a shotgun, or a single pistol. The infantry were somewhat better armed, and the artillery consisted of a four-gun battery and Captain Hiram Bledsoe's three-gun battery, the latter containing the famous cannon "Old Sacramento," so called because it had been captured during the Mexican War at the Battle of Sacramento.

Early on the morning of July 5 Sigel marched north from Carthage, while Jackson broke camp at Lamar and started south at the same time. About eight miles from Carthage just north of Dry Fork, Sigel's forward column encountered Captain Jo Shelby's armed cavalrymen in advance of the State Guard. When Sigel saw his forward column checked, he sent two companies of infantry and two artillery pieces to support them. Shelby then withdrew to the main body of state troops, and each side formed into a line of battle. Behind the State Guard's main line, the 2,000 unarmed cavalrymen, forming what Shelby called the "line of spectators," were arranged to appear as a reserve force.[4]

At about 9:00 a.m. Sigel's big guns opened fire. Captain Bledsoe's three-gun battery answered with legendary accuracy. The peculiar clink of Old Sacramento rang out across the battlefield, and eight Union soldiers reportedly fell dead. Old Sac's second barrage was said to have scored a direct hit on one of Sigel's cannon, completely destroying it.[5]

As the artillery guns blasted away at each other, Rains' unarmed cavalrymen, keeping their distance to conceal their lack of weapons, moved off to the side in a flanking action that posed as a threat. At the same time Shelby's rangers and some of the other armed cavalry flanked Sigel on the opposite side in an attempt to cut off his supply train. Sigel had little respect for the fighting ability of the untrained state troops, but, perceiving that he was greatly outnumbered, the seasoned Union commander began a grudging withdrawal.

After fording Dry Fork, his rear guard made a stand on the south bank of the creek, firing repeated salvos across the stream as the pursuing State Guard scurried along the opposite bank trying to find an alternate place to cross. Many of the day's casualties fell here at the creek during the heated, two-hour exchange, and thus the engagement became known by Confederates as the Battle of Dry Fork.

Sigel dropped back a second time only after a sufficient number of state troops had made it across the stream to again flank his position and threaten his wagon train. Another skirmish occurred at Buck Branch, where Sigel had to fight his way through an enemy line that had managed to surround him. Continuing his methodical retreat, he made another stand at the crossing of Spring River, slowing the pursuit of the state troops and forcing them to seek other points along the river to ford the deep water. During the delay, Colonel John T. Hughes, who was among the officers leading the State Guard advance, took time out from war to admire the aesthetic beauty of the river. Writing home the next day, he pronounced it "the handsomest stream I ever beheld."[6]

Fighting resumed south of the river, where the State Guard pressed the Yankees into Carthage and through the streets of the town. In Carthage, according to General W. Y. Slack of the Missouri State Guard's Fourth Division, the "stand of the enemy was an obstinate one...," with the Union soldiers "taking shelter in and behind houses, walls, and fences."[7]

As the Federals fell back east of Carthage, they made one last stand near the springs where they'd camped the night before. Then darkness finally enabled Sigel to break contact with the pursuing Rebels and withdraw from the running battle that had lasted all day. He and his exhausted troops retired to Sarcoxie eighteen miles away.

Gauged against the monumental clashes of the Civil War such as Antietam, Gettysburg, and Shiloh, the engagement at Carthage was a mere skirmish. Union casualties numbered about 15 dead and 35 wounded while the state troops lost approximately twice as many. The battle was important, however, because of its status as one of the first land battles of the war and because of its strategic significance.

All eyes were on Missouri during the spring and early summer of 1861 as a divided nation watched to see which side would prevail in the struggle between Governor Jackson and General Lyon for the state. When word of the fighting at Carthage reached the East, the news was greeted with exaggerated ado, and the event made headlines in newspapers across the country. A front-page banner in the July 11 New York Times called the Carthage engagement a "Great Battle in Missouri."[8]

Despite greater losses on the side of the State troops, the Battle of Carthage was a strategic victory for the South. Colonel Sigel had failed in his mission to cut off a juncture between the State Guard and General McCulloch's army in Arkansas, and the Union withdrawal gave the Confederacy temporary control of the southwest corner of Missouri.

On the same day as the Battle of Carthage, the Rebels scored another coup when Arkansas Confederates from General McCulloch's and General N. Bart Pearce's commands, on their way north to rescue Governor Jackson, swept into Neosho and captured without resistance the company of 137 men left there by Sigel.

General Price, marching from his camp in the extreme southwest corner of Missouri with a contingent of state troops, arrived in Carthage too late to take part in the fighting but in time to join in the Confederate celebration. Then, with his full command of Missouri State Guardsmen, he dropped back down to Cowskin Prairie in McDonald County, the site he'd selected to train his raw recruits.

2
Jim Lane and the Skirmish at
Dry Wood Creek

After the bitter border struggle of the 1850s that led to Kansas's admission to the Union as a free state, many Kansans harbored a keen distrust for their neighboring, slave- holding state of Missouri, and in the days and months leading up to the Civil War, they kept a wary eye on the political fight in Missouri over the question of secession. After Missouri Governor Jackson's call for state troops to resist General Lyon's Federal army, the wariness of Kansans turned to panic. Kansas Governor Charles Robinson saw Governor Jackson's proclamation as a virtual declaration of war, and he called on the people of his state to organize militia companies to defend against a possible invasion from Missouri.[1]

Kansas citizens flocked to the border area ready to repulse the feared attack. Many, though, were unwilling to adopt a purely defensive strategy. Most of the young men in western Missouri had left their homes to follow Price during the early stages of the war, and Kansans such as Charles R. "Doc" Jennison and James Montgomery saw in the unguarded border an opportunity to punish their neighboring state for its secessionist zeal and for the misdeeds of border ruffians dating back to the days of "Bleeding Kansas."[2] Deciding that the best way to prevent an invasion of Kansas was to keep the Missourians occupied defending their home state, Jennison, Montgomery, and others raided across the border during the summer of 1861 at the head of irregular bands, burning homes and barns and harassing Missouri citizens, Unionist and secessionist alike.

Prior to the war, Jennison, a physician from New York, had gathered around him a band of followers from the Mound City area. He and his gang ranged throughout Southern Kansas driving proslavery settlers out of the territory at the point of a gun. In June of

1861, after the outbreak of war, Jennison crossed into Missouri and raided up and down the border area from Rich Hill to Kansas City, plundering homes, tormenting citizens, and even murdering in at least one instance.[3]

Also from the Mound City area, Montgomery, a Methodist minister and radical abolitionist, had been a leader in the free-state movement in Kansas from the territory's earliest days, and in 1858 he raided across the border with a party led by John Brown on a mission to liberate slaves. Shortly after Jennison's raid at the outset of the war, Montgomery led a foray of his own into Missouri and came back loaded down with plunder and accompanied by a number of slaves he had set free.

Jennison and Montgomery were joined by other leaders like Daniel R. Anthony, brother of Susan B. Anthony; Marshall Cleveland, an ex-convict whose band was little more than a gang of criminals; John Brown, Jr., son of the fanatic abolitionist; and John B. Stewart in conducting raids throughout the remainder of the year and into early 1862 on communities like Butler, Dayton, Harrisonville, Morristown, Papinsville, Pleasant Hill, and West Point in Bates and Cass counties. Many members of these bands were Unionist refugees who'd been forced out of Missouri because of their views and who, therefore, nursed a special hatred toward their former state.

During mid-August 1861, Kansas's newly elected senator, James H. Lane, arrived on the scene in southern Kansas to take charge of the irregular bands and try to form them and other recruits into some semblance of a regular army. The senator had earlier received a Federal commission as a brigadier general that he'd been forced through political pressure to relinquish. Although he'd then obtained a commission from the governor of his home state of Indiana, he was acting without official Federal or Kansas military authority when he arrived at Fort Scott. The question of Senator Lane's legal military status, however, had little to do with the fact that most Missourians viewed his and other "jayhawking" bands throughout the war with the same disdain that Kansans held for Missouri bushwhackers.

Lane had been in southern Kansas only a week when he sent a letter to Fort Leavenworth suggesting that he meant to "play hell with Missouri."[4] A day or two later, he learned that a force of Rebels under Colonel Thomas Cummins of Bates County was at Balltown in north central Vernon County, where they had seized McNeil's mill and pressed it into service to supply Missouri State Guard troops. True to his word, Lane sent Captain James Williams of Montgomery's regiment to "play hell" with the novice millers.

Just outside the village, Williams skirmished with a detachment of the Rebels, killing two, and he chased Cummins's whole force south to the Marmaton River. The next day Williams came back and burned McNeil's Mill and the bridge over the Osage. He then collected the slaves of the mill owner and a sizeable herd of livestock and headed back to Kansas.

Meanwhile, Senator Lane was busy moving most of his arms and supplies from Fort Scott to Fort Lincoln about twelve miles to the north on the Little Osage, a post that he felt could be better defended than Fort Scott.

*****

General Price spent two weeks at Cowskin Prairie drilling and equipping his raw soldiers for war. The army was outfitted, at least in part, through horses, weapons, and equipment impressed from private citizens. A Union report complained of the "general system of outlawry" existing in southwest Missouri during late July and early August in which Southern soldiers were given commissions or "furloughs to hunt" that amounted to little more than licenses to plunder and steal from "friend and foe alike." According to the report, "The people are fleeing from these terrible evils that afflict them at home, and are seeking asylum among utter strangers."[5]

After outfitting his army, General Price marched toward Springfield around the first of August 1861. On the way, he was informed of disturbances to his rear in Vernon and other western Missouri counties, but he postponed a response in deference to more pressing matters at hand. On the 10th of August, he and McCulloch met General Lyon's Union army at the Battle of Wilson's Creek, where Lyon was killed and the Confederates carried the day.

Price now turned his attention to the intelligence from Vernon County. Shortly after the battle, he sent General Rains "to clear the counties bordering upon Kansas of the marauding and murdering bands that infested that section of the State."[6] Senator Lane was just beginning to organize and deploy his "Kansas Brigade" as Rains started from Springfield.

Senator James H. Lane organized the Kansas Brigade. Courtesy *J. Dale West Collection*

On August 25 Price and the remainder of his command started north from Springfield toward the Missouri River, where the general planned to establish a camp to accept new recruits from the northern part of the state. At Bolivar he received a message from Rains that Kansas raiders had burned McNeil's Mill and the bridge over the Osage. Rains also stated that the Federals were gathering in such force at Fort Scott that he couldn't defeat them without reinforcements.

Price turned westward with his whole army and marched for Vernon County. During the trip, according to Colonel John T. Hughes of the State Guard's Fourth Division, the Missouri troops "found the country for twenty miles laid waste, the inhabitants plundered, several persons killed, and the people in much alarm for their safety."[7] Price camped on the evening of the 31st of August three miles west of Nevada.

The next morning, Sunday, September 1, he sent a scout of about 800 men under General A. E. Steen to reconnoiter the enemy. The main force of the patrol took up a concealed position behind a high ridge not far from Fort Scott while an advance of about 200 men under Colonel Benjamin Rives proceeded toward the very edge of the Federal installation.

General Lane had about 1,800 men at Fort Scott, consisting of three regiments under Colonels James Montgomery, William Weer, and Hamilton P. Johnson. In addition there were two artillery pieces, one of them a twelve-pound mountain howitzer manned by regular army sergeant Thomas Moonlight, who was quickly promoted to captain and later in the war rose to the rank of brigadier general. Jennison and his "Independent Rangers" were also stationed at nearby Barnesville.

The Federals were holding Sunday morning religious services in a grove in the valley of the Marmaton River, and hundreds of soldiers, leaving their main camps virtually deserted, were in attendance. The preacher was Colonel Montgomery, and, according to the 1887 *History of Vernon County*,

> He was holding forth in eloquent terms upon the necessity of repentance and baptism for the remission of sins. This man of war was preaching the gospel of peace, with his sword upon his thigh and his Bible in his hand. But just over the hill, a mile or so away, were a lot of Sabbath-breakers and disturbers of religious worship.[8]

Some of the Union soldiers who were not in church were tending a large number of Federal horses and mules that had been turned out to graze on the prairie grass along the river bottoms. Suddenly Colonel Rives's men swept down upon the herd nearest to them, which consisted of about 100 mules belonging to Weer's regiment. The Rebels, "yelling like Comanches" according to the county history, got between the herd and the camps, scattered the herders, and drove between 90 and 100 mules into Missouri and eventually into Price's camp. Thus the action at Dry Wood Creek is sometimes called the Battle of the Mules.

When the Federals attending the church service saw and heard the commotion, according to the county history, "The meeting was adjourned summarily, without the doxology or the benediction." Perceiving that "the rebel Philistines were upon them...,"

Montgomery quickly lay "aside his sacerdotal robes and buckeled on his revolvers...."[9]

About 500 Federals from Johnson and Montgomery's regiments sprang to their saddles and chased after the mule thieves until they reached the top of the ridge and saw Steen's detachment of 800 Rebels facing them from the bottom of the hill. The Union colonels maneuvered to try to draw the Missouri troops into an engagement, and several shots were exchanged. Steen, though, had already accomplished his mission of determining the strength and location of the enemy, and he promptly withdrew toward Price's camp. Casualties in the brief skirmish were light on both sides. Colonel Hughes of the State Guard placed the Federal loss at three or four killed and several wounded, and he claimed the Missourians had none killed and only four wounded.

Steen returned to camp with his intelligence, and the next day, Price's entire command, reinforced by troops from north of the Missouri River, marched about six or seven miles toward Fort Scott and stopped near the banks of Dry Wood Creek.

The same day, September 2, Lane's cavalry went out in pursuit of the Rebels and the lost mules. Some of the State Guard were carelessly chatting and eating apples out of an orchard along the road when the Kansans under Montgomery and Weer, about 500 men, met Price's advance under General Steen on the prairie west of Dry Wood Creek. A party of Federals swooped down on the idlers, cutting them off from their comrades, and three or four Missouri troops were captured. As Montgomery and the Federals came on, Steen re-crossed Dry Wood and dropped back to the crest of a hill east of the creek, then sent word to General Price of the enemy's presence. Montgomery followed across the stream and formed in a line in the tall prairie grass at the edge of the creek timber.

Price came up to the top of the hill with that portion of his forces that were nearest the scene of action and personally took charge of the engagement. He sent back for the artillery battery under Captain Bledsoe and formed a battle line along the ridge with the big guns in the middle. He dispatched General Steen with a body of cavalry to cross the creek downstream and flank the enemy.

Captain Moonlight opened up with his short cannon, firing so rapidly and effectively that the Missouri troops momentarily mistook the single artillery piece for a whole battery. Bledsoe answered with Old Sac and his two other guns. The grape and canister from the

Rebel guns "whistled fearfully over the heads" of the Union soldiers and "went tearing through the trees and brush" behind them, but did little actual damage.[10]

Throughout the skirmish the artillery did most of the fighting on both sides, but some of the infantry of the State Guard got involved during a lull in the artillery fire after Bledsoe and some of his cannoneers fell wounded. According to the Vernon County history, "A brisk little skirmish now began."[11] When the infantry of the State Guard crept forward to open fire, many of the Federals dismounted at the edge of the timber and returned fire. General Price himself rode out to the front but, according to the county history, did not attract much attention because "in his plain dress he could not be distinguished from an old farmer."[12]

Soon Captain Henry Guibor's four-gun battery came up to reinforce Bledsoe, and the cannonade resumed. For several minutes, says the county history, "the firing was hot and spirited."[13]

Price was unable to determine the strength of the enemy because of their concealed position in the tall grass, and, therefore, hesitated to attack, despite overwhelming odds in his favor. Colonel Hughes complained bitterly after the skirmish that he "could not see very many of the enemy, sometimes seeing the muzzles of their guns above the high grass and occasionally the tops of their heads. They will not fight in open fields."[14]

The time involved in bringing up the State Guard's straggling rear and the lively fire of Moonlight's howitzer also contributed to the delay in an assault by the Missouri troops. When Price finally determined that the body facing him was no more than one-fifth the strength of the force he already had at the front, not counting the several thousand additional troops he had in reserve at the rear, he ordered an advance, and the Federals quickly retired from the fray.

Steen's cavalry pursued the fleeing Yankees for about three miles before approaching darkness prompted a halt to the chase. The retreat of the Federals, like their discreet position in the tall grass, aroused a note of acrimony in Colonel Hughes, who complained, "A large army had just as well pursue a lot of 'Arabs' as these Kansas jayhawkers," and he called the withdrawal "the cowardly flight of Senator James Lane and Montgomery."[15]

The skirmish, which lasted a little over an hour, produced minimal casualties. Senator Lane reported five of his men killed and six wounded and said of the enemy toll only that the Missouri troops had "suffered considerably."[16] General Price put his loss at two killed and twenty-three wounded. He reported burying three Federals and suggested, "Many others were doubtless left dead in the rank grass...."[17]

When Senator Lane learned that Price's entire army, consisting of upwards of 10,000 men, was in the area, he withdrew to Fort Lincoln but left about 450 cavalrymen to cover his retreat or, in Lane's own words, "to amuse the enemy."[18]

Instead they plundered the town. Fort Scott had been virtually deserted as soon as its citizens learned that thousands of Rebel troops lay just across the border, but apparently the townspeople had as much to fear from their own soldiers as they did from Price. The principle of defending Missouri's borders upon which the general had acted at the onset of hostilities still guided his conduct of the war, and he declined to invade the state of Kansas. Content at having merely chastised Lane and driven him from Fort Scott, Price spent several days bogged down on Dry Wood Creek by heavy rains before heading north toward Lexington, which he captured later in September after a three-day siege.

Jennison arrived from Barnesville too late to take part in the skirmishing at Dry Wood but in time to join in the pillaging of Fort Scott. After the departure of the Rebel army, he and Colonel Johnson trailed the Rebel army as far as Papinsville and came back loaded down with plunder and a number of "contrabands" or liberated slaves.[19]

3
The Raid on Osceola and the
Burning of Humboldt

Shortly after the beginning of the war, John B. Matthews, a former trader among the Osage at White Hair's Village (later Little Town and now Oswego), was commissioned by General McCulloch to enlist Indians to operate for the Confederacy on the Kansas frontier. Matthews, who had married an Osage woman, held great sway among the tribes, and he successfully recruited a number of Osage, Quapaw, and Cherokee to the Southern cause. According to Indian agent Augustus Wattles (a former associate of John Brown), Matthews raided throughout southeast Kansas in 1861 "committing depredations at the head of a band of half breed Cherokees all summer."[1]

Kansas newspapers claimed that more than half the gang was actually composed of whites from southwest Missouri and northwest Arkansas, but they agreed with Wattles that Matthews was a common outlaw. He and his men had reportedly killed at least sixteen settlers in southeast Kansas and, in addition, had threatened the community of Humboldt during August and driven as many as sixty Union families from their homes in the area.[2]

On the afternoon of September 9, Matthews rode into Humboldt at the head of his motley band to carry out his month-old threat. Although most of his men were white, many tried to disguise themselves to look like Indians. His force was bolstered by a company of Missourians under Tom Livingston of Jasper County, making a total force of about 125 men, but reinforcements were hardly necessary. The town had been left utterly defenseless, because most of the Allen County men of fighting age had gone to Fort Lincoln under a local militia colonel, Allen Thurston, to join Senator Lane's Kansas Brigade. At the time of the raid, another local citizen, Dr. George A. Miller, had been trying to organize a home guard force among the old men and boys of the community, but it was not yet in place.[3]

Matthews and his men swept into Humboldt without resistance and threw a guard around the town to prevent anyone from leaving. Several men who tried to escape were fired at to deter their flight, but no one was injured. The raiders announced that they had come after John Gilmore and that no women, children, or private homes would be molested. Gilmore, a former merchant at the Osage Mission (where St. Paul is now located) had been a business associate of Livingston and was related to Matthews by marriage. However, he did not share their Southern sympathies, and he had recently moved his family and his stock of goods to Humboldt to try to avoid being drawn into the war. The raiders announced that they were there to take back his merchandise, some of which supposedly belonged to Livingston.[4]

Apparently, the one exception to their pledge not to bother private residences was the dwelling of Colonel Thurston. The raiders promptly called at the home and robbed it of everything of value, including Mrs. Thurston's silver spoons, gold watch, breast pin, and other jewelry. Two or three times they tried to set fire to the house, but the colonel's wife kept extinguishing the blaze until they finally gave up. The Rebels demanded that Mrs. Thurston reveal the whereabouts of her Negro servant girl, but she steadfastly refused, even when one of the raiders pulled out his pistol, put it to her head, and threatened to blow her brains out if she didn't divulge the girl's hiding place.[5]

Although the young housemaid eluded capture, other members of her family were not so fortunate. The raiders found twelve members of the family living in a nearby house and captured them for the purpose of taking them back across the state line. Although one Union observer described the family as "free Negroes," another allowed that they were "probably fugitives from Missouri."[6]

Some of the member of Matthews's band cut down the town flag pole, and "a fiendish shout went up for Jeff Davis and the Southern Confederacy." Some of the Rebels tore the Union banner into pieces and "adorned themselves with strips of the streamer."[7]

Meanwhile, the work of plundering the town's businesses went on. The raiders took all the money and valuables they could lay their hands on, including an estimated $1,500 in goods from the store of Coffey and Marsh alone. They loaded the loot and the captives, consisting of Gilmore and the black family, into two wagons, which they pressed into service, and they also stole fourteen horses from in and around the town. The Rebels then retreated southward, harassing and robbing settlers along the way.[8]

The raid spurred the rapid organization of Humboldt's fledgling home guard, and Lane promptly "offered a reward of $1,000 for the head of Matthews."[9] He also sent Lieutenant Colonel (later General) James G. Blunt of Montgomery's regiment to take charge of the new company at Humboldt and pursue the robbers. With a combined force of about 200 men, Blunt set out after Matthews into Indian country south of Humboldt. On the morning of September 18, the Federals came upon Matthews and his band sixty guerrillas camped at a home near present-day Chetopa. When the Rebels made a dash for their horses in a nearby corral, the Federals immediately opened fire. Matthews and about ten of his men were killed in the initial fire, while the rest managed to escape. Blunt seized about fifty horses and ponies, 200 buffalo robes, and other loot, most of which he turned over to the volunteers from Allen County in payment for their service. On Matthews's body was found an order from General McCulloch authorizing Matthews to organize and enlist the Quapaw Indians.[10]

In the meantime, General Lane with about 1,500 men set out north along the border, in the wake of Price's retreat from Dry Wood, with plans to "pitch into Butler, Harrisonville, and Papinsville."[11] Also on his list of targets were Clinton and Osceola. He reached Trading Post in Linn County on September 12, turned east into Missouri, and began plundering and burning. The next day his cavalry "cleared out Butler and Parkville," and on the 14th the march reached West Point in the northwest corner of Bates County.[12]

From there he sent an expedition under Colonels Montgomery and Johnson into Cass County. The Kansas troops overran and laid waste the village of Morristown, but Johnson was killed by a hastily organized home guard during the initial attack.[13]

While at West Point, Lane also issued a lengthy proclamation, dated September 19, 1861, to the people of western Missouri. He sought to assure the people that he did not countenance the lawless depredations that had been committed on the property of Missouri citizens and that he would make an effort to redress their grievances if they would demonstrate their loyalty. He cautioned the people against joining or supporting the guerrilla bands that had formed for the ostensible purpose of protecting Missouri and suggested that the best way for the people to protect themselves against plunderers from either Kansas or Missouri was to stand firm with the Union, because of its superiority in numbers, arms, equipment, money, and "everything necessary to carry on war."[14]

Then, in a statement that rather belied his condemnation of lawless pillaging, Lane went on to justify the stealing of Missouri property that had thus far occurred by suggesting that it had only happened because the people of western Missouri were in arms against the government. "Be not afraid of Kansas...," he told the people, "unless you engage in this wicked rebellion inaugurated by that restless State, the maker of all mischief—South Carolina."[15]

After urging the people to tend to their lawful pursuits and asking influential citizens to join together to try to break up the guerrilla bands, the senator ended his decree with a grim warning:

> Should you, however, disregard my advice, the stern visitations of war will be meted out to the rebels and their allies. I shall then be convinced that your arming for protection is a sham, and rest assured that the traitor, where caught, shall receive a traitor's doom. The cup of mercy has been exhausted. Treason hereafter will be treated as treason. The two roads are open to you. People of western Missouri, choose ye between them; the one will lead you to peace and plenty, the other to destruction."[16]

From West Point, Lane turned back to the southeast and marched down the Marais des Cygnes River to Papinsville, where, according to at least one report, he had a desperate skirmish with a sizeable Rebel force on September 21. The Federals lost seventeen killed and a large number wounded, while the Rebels purportedly lost forty killed and a hundred taken prisoner.[17]

From Papinsville, Lane followed the Osage River valley eastward and reached Osceola in St. Clair County on the night the 21st.[18] Although most of the State Guard had gone north with Price, a company of about fifty men under Captain John M. Weidemeyer was in the vicinity of Osceola and learned of Lane's approach. They lay in ambush in some brush at the edge of town and fired a few random pot shots at the Federals, then quickly fell back and took refuge in some of the buildings of the town.[19]

26

Historical marker on courthouse grounds at Osceola commemorating Lane's raid on the town.

The Kansas Brigade spent the night at the edge of Osceola, then advanced on the town the next morning. Captain Moonlight opened up on the courthouse with artillery fire, driving Weidemeyer and his men out of Osceola. One of the cannon shells reportedly hit a building that was used as an ordnance for Price's army, and the structure and its contents went up in a terrible explosion, which, according to the *History of Vernon County*, killed half a dozen civilians.[20] The Rebels beat a hasty retreat toward Warsaw, and two companies of Colonel Weer's men pursued them for about a mile before calling off the chase.

Back in Osceola, Lane's men went to work sacking the town. They broke open the doors of the bank, dragged the safe into the streets, and blew it open. Inside they found only a few worthless private papers, because the bankers, anticipating the possibility of just such a raid as this, had already removed the deposits, totaling over $150,000, to other towns. The empty safe incited Lane's anger, according to the 1883 *History of Henry and St. Clair Counties*, and the plundering of the town began in earnest.

The jayhawkers combed the town, appropriating anything of value. Many objects that were of little worth or too large for convenient removal they tossed into the streets. They broke into the courthouse and destroyed county records. They discovered fifty to a hundred barrels of whiskey, which the officers ordered destroyed. The men knocked open the barrels, poured out the contents, and set the liquid ablaze, the liquor running in flaming rivulets in the streets, but not before many of the Kansans had managed to get roaring drunk. They emptied dozens of kegs of molasses until, according to the *History of Vernon County*, "the gutters ran ankle deep with 'black-strap.'"[21]

Nearly every downtown building and a number of dwellings were then put to the torch. "The business portion of the town was a seething mass of flames," says the *History of Henry and St. Clair Counties.*[22]

With the town thoroughly pillaged and burned to the ground, Lane loaded his wagon train with nearly a million dollars' worth of spoils for the trip back to Kansas. In addition to the valuables he had seized, he also carried off a number of slaves whom he'd liberated during the raid. The author of the *History of Henry and St. Clair Counties* complained that "Negroes swarmed to Lane like flies around a carcass, and were permitted to load themselves down with goods of every description."[23]

In his report of the Osceola incident written on the 24th, Lane admitted that, after the Rebels took shelter in the downtown buildings, "We were compelled to shell them out, and in doing so the place was burned to ashes...." He further stated that fifteen to twenty of the enemy were killed or wounded, but he gave no indication as to whether any of them were civilians. Lane's report says that the Federals sustained no losses during the raid. In a separate letter to General John C. Fremont also dated the 24th, Lane justified his march on Osceola by pointing out that "It was the depot of the traitors for Southwestern Missouri." He cited the destruction of Price's ammunition storehouse as the primary purpose of the raid, but whether such a depot even existed is questionable. Lane's real motivation was plunder, the liberation of slaves, and the political dividends that a foray into secessionist western Missouri might pay back in Kansas.[24]

*****

After Humboldt's home guard helped track down John Matthews, the man responsible for plundering the town in early September, the local force, numbering about 100 men, kept a vigil for a couple of weeks in anticipation of another possible invasion. Cavalry scouting parties regularly patrolled the area surrounding the town, and the infantry, although allowed to stay in their homes, remained on alert. By early October, though, the scouts had been called off and the cavalry sent home. Once again the town let down its guard.

In the late afternoon of October 14th, about 300 cavalrymen of the Eleventh Regiment Missouri State Guard under Colonel A.J. Talbott of Jasper County galloped into Humboldt and seized the town before Dr. Miller, captain of the scattered home guard, could organize a defense. The raiders celebrated their coup with random gunfire as they rode through the streets of the town. A few bystanders managed to escape by fleeing upon first sight of the horsemen, but most of the men of the town were quickly captured and placed under guard.[26]

Dr. Miller, presuming that he would be summarily shot if he surrendered, was among the last to give up his arms. Finally, though, he handed over his guns with a mere plea that the women and children be spared.

Colonel Talbott then ordered the town put to the torch. Not only, though, did he spare the women and children, but he allowed them to remove valuables and household goods from their homes before the dwellings were fired and he directed his men to help in the removal. He further astonished the doctor by not executing the male prisoners.

Several buildings, including the churches and the Masonic Hall, were also spared. Another structure that was saved was the home of Dr. William Wakefield, who, when he saw that resistance was futile, invited the Rebel officers to have supper with him. Among those who reportedly took him up on the offer was Tom Livingston, whose Jasper County guerrillas had again come along for the frolic. A few residences, where the female occupants claimed to be too sick to be moved, were spared also, and a few other

29

structures such as the courthouse and one of the general stores, which were set on fire, were extinguished before being burned to the ground. The rest of the town, however, was reduced to ashes.

The Rebels rounded up all the horses they could find but stole very little other property. The only person killed was a man named Seachrist who was shot when he ignored an order to halt while trying to make a getaway with his mules.

The raiders galloped out of town shortly after dark, leaving Humboldt still in flames. At the edge of town they released their captives, who returned in time to help save a couple of burning structures.

The sacking of Humboldt was a quick-hit raid of narrow purpose. The Rebels stayed only a short while, and they destroyed no property coming and going. Rebel leaders supposedly told citizens of the town that Humboldt was burned in reprisal for the killing of Matthews and the sacking and burning of Osceola, and the single-mindedness of the mission seems to confirm that the raid was designed as a retaliatory strike.

The *History of Vernon County* poignantly suggests the growing flavor of revenge that suffused the hostilities along the Missouri-Kansas border by the fall of 1861:

> Lane's men claimed that they burned Osceola because the rebel raiders had robbed and plundered Humboldt. Col. Talbott's men claimed they burned Humboldt in retaliation for the burning of Osceola. Then Lane's men burned Dayton, Morristown, and other Missouri villages in retaliation for the burning of Humboldt, and so it went on.[27]

4
The War in Bates County and the Skirmish at Island Mound

After Lane's raid on Osceola, other Missourians besides those who burned Humboldt also retaliated. On October 29, 1861, Sheriff John Clem of Bates County led a "posse" of forty men across the border into Linn County under the pretext of recovering property taken from Missouri. Arriving at the home of Richard Manning on Mine Creek, the Rebels "informed him that he had to die." When the frightened Manning sprang for his gun, the gang promptly shot him dead. At the same house, the Missourians also found a young man named William Upton lying in bed. They shot and killed him before he could get up and then robbed the premises of everything of value.[1]

As the raiders approached the home of Thomas Speakes, Joseph Speakes saw them coming and slipped away to alert his neighbors. After rounding up about twenty horses and two wagons from the neighborhood, the raiders started back to Missouri. Meanwhile, though, in response to Speakes's alarm, a party of fourteen Union men had armed themselves and taken up a position on the road leading out of Kansas. When the Rebels approached, the Union men opened fire, killing two and wounding several of the raiders. The Missourians returned fire, killing Joseph Speakes and slightly wounding a couple of other Union men, before making their escape. The Rebels were pursued into Missouri but to no avail.[2]

A day or two later, an unknown party of Missourians made a foray into Linn County and killed a man named Smith at Brooklin, a small village in the northern part of the county. They also stole four wagons and twenty-four horses. Then on the morning of November 12, another band of Missourians from around Butler crossed into Linn County, killed a man named James Sage, and wounded two others. Apparently Sage was targeted because he was a Union man who had previously lived in Missouri and had fled at the state at the start of the war.[3]

Around the middle of November, a party of Kansas citizens from the neighborhood of Mound City were on their way to Osceola with wagons and teams to procure their winter's supply of salt when they were attacked near Butler in Bates County by "two companies of secessionists...led on by the notorious Sheriff Clem." The Unionists claimed to have killed nine Rebels before making "the best retreat they could."[4]

On November 20, 1861, Sidney Jackman, captain of a cavalry company in the Missouri State Guard, attacked "a hundred robbers from Kansas" about four miles east of Butler, as the plunderers were on their way home with their loot, and chased them clear across the border. Newspaper reports at the time suggested that the jayhawkers were "completely stripped of their plunder and badly cut up," with about a half dozen men missing and presumed dead. In recalling the incident years later, Jackman boasted that he recovered nearly all the stolen property and killed as many as forty Kansans, while his own loss was just "one old horse wounded."[5]

In early December, Clem, who was also a Missouri State Guard officer, made another raid into Linn County leading a band of men estimated between 100 and 300. The gang plundered the community of Potosi and burned grain and buildings in the area. When the raiders called at the home of Josiah Sykes, located just north of the village, he escaped and, while barefooted and dressed just in his pants, "made the best possible time over the frozen ground" toward Mound City. Later, the gang shot at least one citizen, an old man named Seright whom they ordered to produce a firebrand so that they could burn his stacks of hay. According to a Union report, the seventy-two-year-old man brought out some burning sticks from his fireplace as ordered, but the raiders shot him in the back nonetheless and "burned every thing combustible on the place."[6]

When Sykes reached Mound City with news of the raid, Colonel Montgomery promptly sent a detachment of about 700 troops under Major H.H. Williams in pursuit of the marauders. However, the Missourians dispersed before they could be tracked down, and Williams discharged his frustration by burning the town of Papinsville on the night December 13. After the women and children were provided for, "in the choice and expressive language of Jim Lane, Papinsville 'went up.'"[7]

Next Williams sent Captain John E. Stewart's cavalry fifteen miles away to burn the county seat at Butler. Reaching the place on the afternoon of December 14, Stewart fired the courthouse and all the business section of the town. While Butler was still burning, Jackman and his guerrillas rode in and drove the Federals out of town, killing at least two of Stewart's men. On their retreat to Kansas, the Federal troops destroyed homes and confiscated stock all along their path, and a number of Unionist refugees followed the caravan out of Missouri.[8]

Meanwhile, Montgomery had moved his headquarters from Mound City to a spot nearer the border and boldly dubbed it "Camp Defiance." On the afternoon of December 27, he learned of "a Secesh ball" to be held that night at Stump Town on the Butler to Papinsville road and promptly sent an expedition consisting of one company of cavalry and one of infantry "to attend without an invitation." Because of an unexpected delay, the Federals did not arrive until two o'clock in the morning, at which time the Rebels, according to one report, had already performed their closing number called the "Skedaddle Reel." However, a thorough search of the premises and surrounding vicinity resulted in the confiscation of twenty weapons and the capture of four prisoners, including a lieutenant in General Rains's Missouri State Guard.[9]

On New Year's Eve, 1861, word reached the Cass County camp of Lieutenant-Colonel Daniel Anthony, commanding Jennison's regiment of Lane's brigade, that 160 Rebels were occupying Dayton in the southern portion of the county. Anthony and several other officers, including notorious jayhawker George H. Hoyt, took three companies of troops and rode into Dayton just before daylight on New Year's Day. The "bird had flown," but the Rebels had left horses, weapons, and equipment, which the Federals seized. The troops then "applied a Union torch and left the town amidst a lively conflagration."[10]

The Federals pursued the fleeing Rebels to the timber of the Grand River along the northern border of Bates County, where the Rebels fired a volley, killing a Union horse and momentarily checking the pursuit. Resuming the chase, the troops followed the Rebels into Henry County to Big Creek northwest of Clinton near the small community of Wadesburg on the Henry-Cass county line.

Upon their return to Cass County, the Federals reported having killed as many as twenty to thirty Rebels during the running skirmish.[11]

In early 1862, Bates County and the northern part of Vernon County swarmed with guerrillas under William Marchbanks, Sidney Jackman, and others. Marchbanks and Jackman had been sent into the area around the first of the year by General Rains to recruit for the Missouri State Guard with the ostensible purpose of going south to join the Confederacy, but they lingered in the area for several months foraging and bushwhacking. In response to the Rebel activity in the area, a regiment of the First Iowa Cavalry was stationed at Butler around March of 1862, and the guerrillas retired to the dense thickets along the rivers and streams. By mid-May, the Bates County Court had resumed operation, and most of Butler's businesses had recovered from the fire five months earlier. Relative peace had been restored to the county.[12]

Then, on May 17, 1862, a detachment of the First Iowa Cavalry went on a foraging expedition southwest of Butler and came back with two wagon loads of corn taken from the farm of Oliver Elswick. In response, a local guerrilla leader named William "Bill" Turman, who had his headquarters on a nearby island of the Marais Des Cygnes River (sometimes called Hog Island), collected his men to determine, according to the county history, "what should be done about the d-----d Federals for hauling away our corn." Before daylight the next morning, the bushwhackers rode toward Butler and lay in ambush at the crossing of Miami Creek in anticipation of the foraging party returning in quest of more corn. Sure enough, shortly after daybreak, two mule-drawn Federal wagons started out of Butler along the road toward the Elswick farm. When the wagons paused at the Miami Creek crossing, the guerrillas sprang up and opened fire, killing three soldiers. Two managed to escape, but by the time a Federal scout from Butler arrived on the scene, the bushwhackers had fled. The three dead soldiers were buried in a small cemetery east of the courthouse square in Butler and later reinterred at the national cemetery in Fort Scott.[13]

Marchbanks was captured in the spring of 1862 about the time the Iowa troops first appeared on the scene, but Jackman lingered in the border area throughout much of the summer, making his principal headquarters near Papinsville, where he had lived at the time of the 1860 census. On the night of August 3, a band of Rebels, supposed to be some of Jackman's men, made their appearance at the Choteau trading post, just across the Kansas line from Bates County. They robbed a store of about $800 worth of goods and fired several errant shots at a young man who happened to be in the store.[14]

As early as 1861, abolitionist Jim Lane had urged the enlistment of blacks into the Federal army, but the Lincoln administration balked at this radical step. Lane nevertheless began recruiting blacks the following year and organizing the First Kansas Colored Volunteer Infantry. By the fall of 1862, the black troops were ready to be tested, even though they had still not been officially mustered into service.[15]

On October 26, Captain Richard G. Ward, commanding about 160 men of the First Kansas Colored Infantry, and Captain Henry C. Seaman, in charge of another seventy men from the same regiment, combined forces and crossed into Bates County near Hog Island (also called Osage Island) in response to reports of a concentration of Rebel forces in the area. Among the guerrilla leaders assembled in the area was Bill Turman, leader of the ambush party at Miami Crossing the previous spring.[16]

On October 27, according to Captain Ward, the Federals took possession of "old man Toothman's house." This was a reference to Enoch Toothman, whose son John was among the guerrillas gathered on Hog Island, and the father was also known as "a noted rebel guerrilla." The farm's split rail fences were used to erect a hasty breastworks around the house, and a hand-made version of the U.S. flag was put up over the barricade. Consequently, the site is sometimes called "Fort Toothman," and some of the soldiers also referred to it as Fort Africa during their brief stay, although there was never an actual fort at the location.[17]

Almost as soon as the soldiers arrived, the guerrillas began skirmishing with Federal scouts and pickets in an attempt to draw them out, but the soldiers stayed inside the relative safety of their crude citadel. After nightfall, Ward and Seaman dispatched runners back to Kansas requesting reinforcements. On the morning of October 29, with the camp running low on food, Ward sent out a force of about sixty men under Captains Andrew J. Armstrong and Andrew I. Crew to engage the attention of the Rebels while another detachment of about fifty soldiers under Captain Seaman went out foraging. About two miles from camp, the first party came upon

35

some guerrillas and skirmished with them, driving them another two miles from the camp and, according to Ward, "placing seven men hors de combat, with no loss on our side." The bushwhackers, undoubtedly trying to lead the soldiers into a trap, kept shouting racial epithets at the troops and urging them to "come on." The Federals, however, declined the invitation and returned to camp for lunch.[18]

While the soldiers were eating, a small guerrilla force made a charge toward the camp and drove in the Federal pickets but quickly withdrew. Ward then sent out a skirmishing party to retake the picket ground and try to determine the Rebel strength. The Federals drove the guerrillas over a mound south of the Toothman farm and disappeared from Captain Ward's sight. The continued sound of sharp firing concerned the captain, and he promptly sent out another party of about twenty soldiers under Lieutenant Joseph Gardner to reinforce the skirmishers and escort them back to camp.[19]

When neither the skirmishers nor Gardner's party returned promptly, Ward grew anxious, and he and Captain Armstrong went out with yet another force to try to determine the situation. Ward found the guerrillas occupying the mound south of camp and some of his skirmishers off to the west. He also learned that Lieutenant Gardner's detachment was at a house south of the skirmishers making preparations to return to camp. Fearful that the bushwhackers would try to cut Gardner off, Ward ordered Captain Armstrong and his men to flank the guerrillas and try to gain a position at the rear of the mound on which the Rebels were located. Armstrong had just gotten to the other side of the mound when the bushwhackers, numbering over a hundred, charged toward Gardner's party of about twenty-five men, who were on their way back to camp. The soldiers raced over the mound trying to gain a ravine on the north slope, but the guerrillas caught up with them before they could reach the safety of the defile. Forced to make a stand, the small detachment turned upon the Rebels, and "as their guns cracked many a riderless horse swung off to one side."[20]

Despite their stubborn stand, the outnumbered Federals were virtually wiped out. Among the dead was Captain Crew, who had gone out from camp in search of the parties that had been sent out earlier and had linked up with Gardner's detachment. Also, Lieutenant Gardner himself was seriously wounded. According to a Union witness, after Gardner had fallen, "one of these brave sons of the South, discovering that he was not yet dead, dismounted, took his revolver off his disabled body and shot him, as he thought, through the head, saying: 'There, Goddamn you, take that.'" However, the shot just grazed the back of Gardner's head, and he later recovered."[21]

Charging to the rescue, Captain Armstrong soon reached the scene of the fray and "came into the fight like a lion, yelling to his men to follow him, and cursing them for not going faster when they were already on the keen jump." The guerrillas dashed down the north slope of the mound, where they were met by a volley from yet another Union force that had been posted near the camp. Executing a flanking movement, the Rebels then galloped back up the hill and got to the rear of Armstrong's force, where they set the prairie on fire to try to deter a pursuit. However, Armstrong's men charged through the smoke and fire and gave the guerrillas another "terrible volley."[22]

Sign at Battle of Island Mound State Historic Site southwest of Butler

The latest salvo prompted the guerrillas to retire. Despite the fact that Rebel reinforcements were arriving, the bushwhackers had apparently had enough of the First Kansas Colored Infantry. According to Captain Ward, the guerrillas had tested the black troops and "had received an answer to the often mooted question of 'will they fight.'"[23]

37

Federal casualties numbered nine killed and eleven wounded, nearly all of them from Gardner's detachment of twenty-five soldiers that the guerrillas intercepted. Owing to the prairie having been set on fire, the Federals did not immediately find two or three of their dead, and when the bodies were eventually found the next day, they had been scalped. Union reports claimed the guerrillas lost eighteen killed and twenty-five wounded in the skirmishing, and several were also taken prisoner, including John Toothman.[24]

This action, the first engagement of the Civil War in which a black unit fought for the Union, has come to be known as the skirmish at Island Mound. The hill south of the Toothman farm where most of the fighting took place was occasionally called by that name, even during the war, because of its proximity to Hog Island.[25]

The following spring, bushwhackers once again started amassing in the Hog Island area. Around the first of May 1863, two Kansas farmers living on the border who wandered over into Missouri in search of some stray cattle were captured by twelve guerrillas and taken to the island. After being held a couple of days, they were turned loose, but their capture, combined with other Rebel activity in the area, created alarm all along the border and caused mail service between Mound City and Butler to be discontinued.[26]

A week or so later, a detachment of sixty Federal troops made a descent on Hog Island to try to break up the bushwhacking nest and were repulsed. On May 18, another Federal detachment, numbering well over a hundred soldiers, scoured the area and found a large body of guerrillas on the island, where the Rebels had "erected light breastworks, and were preparing for defense." The Union force attacked the encampment and routed the guerrillas, killing three and wounding five, while the Federals lost one man killed. The soldiers also destroyed 2,000 pounds of bacon and a large quantity of corn that the bushwhackers had stored on the island. The Rebels reported that they were part of the command of Benjamin F. Parker, a Confederate colonel who was recruiting a regiment of Partisan Rangers all along the Kansas-Missouri border.[27]

During the spring of 1863, Captain Charles F. Coleman was stationed at Butler with a detachment of the Ninth Kansas Cavalry, but around the middle of June, Coleman was ordered to West Point in the northwest corner of Bates County to guard the border area. As soon as Coleman moved off, with all the Union families who remained in the country accompanying him, the guerrillas rode into

Butler on June 21 and burned a large part of the town. Kansans had sent the town up in flames in December of 1861, and now the bushwhackers moved in a year and half later to take their turn with the torches.[28]

Hog Island continued to be a refuge for bushwhackers throughout the summer of 1863. In late August, a young Union woman from Bates County who had recently fled across the border to Linn County complained, "The pilfering bands of the so-called C.S.A. bushwhackers have again resumed their old stand, the Island, or Island Mound…. They have robbed every family, with the exception of four, on the Missouri side of the Marais des Cygnes or Osage River." The young lady also reported that on August 21 the guerrillas had raided an area east of the trading post in Linn County known as "the valley." The Rebels robbed eight different families, "one after another, taking everything of value they could get their hands on, in the shape of horses, arms and ammunition, bed clothes and little articles too numerous to mention, including combs, of which I suppose they are greatly in need, from the looks of their long, bushy hair." The young woman wondered why more couldn't be done to put an end to the raiding parties. A company of the Ninth Kansas Cavalry stationed at the trading post was, she allowed, "doubtless a brave company of men, but somehow they always appear in pursuit an hour or so after the foe has fled," and the company "has never succeeded in capturing any bushwhackers."[29]

Shortly after this episode, Brigadier-General Thomas Ewing, Jr., commanding the District of the Border, issued his infamous Order Number 11 in response to Quantrill's massacre at Lawrence. The order required all citizens living in Jackson, Cass, Bates, and northern Vernon counties to leave the area or else move to within a mile of a Union military post, and it also dictated that any grain remaining in these counties after fifteen days would be burned. As a result, Bates County was virtually depopulated overnight, and it and the other affected counties became known as the "burnt district."

When a Union officer was sent into Bates County in early March of 1864, he reported that he had traveled over most of the southern portion of the county and that he was "unable to find forage, bushwhacker, or human being…." Later the same month, another officer reported that there was not enough hay or grain in Bates County to sustain his presence there and that it would have to be brought in from adjacent counties. In early April, yet another officer, stationed in southeast Bates, complained that his horses were starving for lack of forage.[30]

Order Number 11 was an extreme measure that produced a political backlash among not only Southern sympathizers but also conservative Unionists, and in the overall campaign against guerrillas it accomplished very little, because the Rebels merely moved their bases of operations elsewhere. At least in Bates County, though, it had produced the desired effect of quashing the civilian support system of the guerrillas and putting an end to bushwhacking. The county, a witness to numerous skirmishes and raids in the early part of the war, was generally quiet after the summer of 1863.

4
John T. Coffee and the
Non-Confederate Rebellion

In the fall of 1861, after Price's victory at the Siege of Lexington, his army fell back to its southwest Missouri stronghold and camped at Neosho. In late October, meeting at the Masonic hall, Governor Jackson's legislature in exile passed an act of secession on behalf of Missouri. As far as many of its citizens were concerned, the state was now part of the Confederacy.

Having installed a provisional state government after Jackson abandoned Jefferson City, the Union did not recognize his legislature in exile, and whether a quorum of legislators was present in Neosho remains a point of debate to this day. In addition, the complete legislature had, months earlier, invested the state convention with full authority to decide the question of secession. Despite these facts, many Southern-leaning Missourians supported the act of secession, and a good portion of Price's army got drunk celebrating it. The general fired off a hundred-gun salute in honor of the ordinance, and the Confederate government readily approved it.

Shortly after the act of secession was passed at Neosho, Price was designated a major general in the Confederate Army, although the appointment was not immediately confirmed. In early March of 1862, he led his State Guard troops into battle at Pea Ridge, Arkansas, alongside General Earl Van Dorn's regular Confederate soldiers. Then, a month after the Southern defeat at Pea Ridge, Price's appointment was confirmed, and he resigned his commission in the Missouri State Guard to join the Confederate Army.

Confederate officials immediately sent him and Van Dorn east of the Mississippi to reinforce the beleaguered Rebel army in Tennessee. Underestimating the strategic importance of Missouri, the South essentially abandoned the state. However, not all of Price's officers followed him into Confederate service. Some remained in the State Guard and stayed to carry on the fight for Missouri. Notable among these in the southwest part of the state was Colonel John T. Coffee.

Coffee, perhaps more than anyone else, embodied the Rebel war effort in southwest Missouri from the time of Price's departure in the spring of 1862 until Jo Shelby's raid into the central part of the state in the fall of 1863. He became, for at least a brief period, the Union's number-one enemy in the Southwest District headquartered at Springfield.

A native of Tennessee, Coffee migrated to southwest Missouri in the early 1840s and practiced law in Greene, Polk, and Dade counties. At the tail end of the Mexican War, he raised a regiment of men from southwest Missouri, but the war ended before they saw service. In 1854 Coffee was elected to the state senate from Polk and Dade counties, but he resigned the post after only a few months to accept a commission as a captain in the First U.S. Army Cavalry Regiment. Because of illness, he also resigned the military commission after just a few months and returned to Dade County.[1]

Around the end of August of 1856, in response to abolitionist activities occurring in Kansas at that time, a meeting of pro-slavery citizens was held at the Dade County courthouse. Coffee, who himself owned at least one slave, addressed the meeting and was among those appointed to draft a resolution supporting "Southern rights." The next year he went into the newspaper business and in 1858 again ran for office. He was elected to the state legislature from Dade County and became speaker of the house. He did not seek reelection in 1860 but instead campaigned unsuccessfully for the Democratic nomination for Missouri secretary of state.[2]

At the outset of the Civil War the forty-four-year-old Coffee raised a regiment in and around Dade County. However, he missed the engagement at Carthage, having been captured by a Union home guard force a few days prior to the action. On July 5, 1861, the very day of the Carthage engagement, the captors arrived in Springfield with their prisoner, "the celebrated Colonel Coffee, who has been riding secessionism rampantly for the past few months." The next day a Union surgeon visited Coffee in his cell, because, the physician explained, the prisoner had "made a requisition on my medical stores for *good brandy*, which I refused him, thinking his accustomed *Bourbon* better fitted for a secession stomach." Coffee was released in late July, presumably in time to participate in the Battle of Wilson's Creek.[3]

On September 16, 1861, Coffee was elected colonel of the Sixth Cavalry Regiment of the Eighth Division, Missouri State Guard.[4] Coffee's unit acted independently much of the time, however, especially after Price went east in the spring of 1862, and often there was little to distinguish his regiment from one of the many guerrilla bands operating throughout the state, except that Coffee's force was larger than the average partisan band. Like the guerrilla companies, Coffee's regiment acted at times as a sort of renegade outfit and was viewed in that light by many Federal officials and even some Confederate.

Coffee drew the special attention of Union officials in February of 1862 when he was reported near Pineville, 500 strong, recruiting more men.[5]

During the next three months Coffee lingered in the tri-border area of southwest Missouri, northwest Arkansas, and the Indian Nation. In late April he made a brief juncture with Confederate colonel Stand Watie's Cherokee regiment in a chase after 200 Federals near Neosho. Described by one of his own officers as "given to dissipation," Coffee proposed another attack, but he and Stand Watie drank themselves into stupors as they pondered the mission. Stand Watie came to and left camp before Coffee could revive enough to renew the war council.[6]

A month later, though, Coffee again hooked up with a portion of Stand Watie's command under Captain Robert C. Parks. On the morning of May 31, acting on intelligence from guerrilla chieftain Tom Livingston, Coffee and Parks discovered 350 to 400 Missouri State Militia cavalry camped at Neosho. All of Parks's men and some of Coffee's dismounted and crept to the very edge of the Union camp before opening fire. The attack took the Federals by total surprise.

Firing off a random volley, they tried to form a line of defense but then broke and ran in confusion as the Rebels advanced. Coffee's mounted troops under Sidney Jackman chased after the fleeing Yankees for several miles, and, according to Stand Watie's report of the incident dated the following day, many of the Federal casualties "were found some distance from Neosho, they having fallen in their flight." Stand Watie placed the number of Federals killed at ten to fifteen and estimated that their loss in wounded was heavy. He said that the lone man killed on the Confederate side belonged to Coffee's regiment.[7]

On June 1 from his camp on Cowskin Prairie in McDonald County, Coffee also filed a report of the action and submitted it to General Rains:

> On yesterday I, with 200 men of my command and 200 of Stand Watie's under Captain Parks, attacked the State forces under John M. Richardson, to the number of 350, completing routing them, killing and wounding at least forty, capturing all their baggage, tents, camp equipage, twelve horses, twenty-one mules, fifty stands of arms, and various other articles too numerous to mention.
>
> The rout was complete.[8]

A report filed the following day, June 2, by Federal brigadier general E. B. Brown, commander of the Southwest Missouri District, conceded Colonel Richardson's loss of equipment and arms, but Brown claimed the total Federal loss in killed, wounded, and missing was only about ten men. Among the wounded was Richardson himself, who had his horse shot out from under him and dislocated his shoulder when the animal fell on him.[9]

After the surprise attack at Neosho, Coffee moved off to Shoal Creek and camped there with Stand Watie. The next evening, June 1, Union intelligence reported Coffee in the area of Sarcoxie with 1,500 men. This estimate of Rebel strength probably included the men under Stand Watie and still might have been exaggerated, but General Brown set sufficient store by the rumor to urge General Schofield that Federal reinforcements be deployed in the direction of Sarcoxie as soon as possible. The Rebel threat, however, remained only that.[10]

Later in June, Coffee followed Rains to the Indian Nation, where the general established at Tahlequah a temporary headquarters for his Eighth Division of the Missouri State Guard. Although still nominally under Rains's command, Coffee, along with guerrilla chieftain Tom Livingston, was "wandering about promiscuously" in the northern part of the Indian Nation during the latter part of June and early July.[11]

About the first week of July 1862, Coffee crossed the Arkansas border and went into camp at Fayetteville, taking with him four Kansas soldiers he'd captured during one of his meanders. On the evening of July 9th, Coffee detailed a squad to take the four prisoners about mile south of town and execute them. According to Jackman, Coffee was so drunk he forgot about having sent out the detail and mistook the sound of the firing squad as enemy guns. Many of the rank and file in Coffee's regiment grew indignant upon learning of the executions, and Jackman took his company and left Coffee's command to join a Confederate regiment camped about eight miles away (even though Jackman claimed the executions were in retaliation for similar misconduct by Federals). Some of Coffee's remaining men followed Jackman's company into Confederate service, but Coffee himself refused to abandon the Missouri State Guard. General Rains, camped nearby, swore bitterly the next morning upon hearing what Coffee had done. Whether he attempted to discipline his subordinate for the indiscretion is unknown, but the wedge between the two men was growing.[12]

Around the end of the month, Coffee re-entered Missouri, having been ordered out of Arkansas, according to one report, for refusing to join the Confederate Army. Coffee's reappearance on the scene caused Brigadier General Brown at Springfield no little consternation. Union spies reported the strength of the Rebel force as high as 1,000 men during its march north, and Coffee was seen at Marionville in Lawrence County on the evening of August 1 with 500 men. The next day he was spotted twelve miles north of there headed for Dade County, and Brown sent out three companies of Enrolled Missouri Militia from Greene County and fifty U.S. cavalry in pursuit.[13]

On the same day, August 2, the disquieted general also issued a circular urging area citizens to join with Union troops in opposing Coffee and driving him out of the district:

> By the combined effort of the military authorities and all good citizens, without regard to their party or political associations, peace and security to person and property were being rapidly restored to this division, when by the entrance into the State of Coffee and his band all the good work of the past two months may be undone unless the people rise in a body to protect their homes and families.
>
> The commanding general therefore calls on the citizens of Missouri to unite with the military to at once drive those bad men from the country. Form companies under the order of the Governor, bring such arms as you have, and report yourselves to the military commanders wherever you find them, and in a few days, with your

assistance, we will drive the marauders from the State and again restore peace and quiet to our distracted borders. The Government will furnish you with ammunition. Arms taken from Coffee's men will be used to arm the militia as far as possible.[14]

4

General Brown issued a proclamation against Coffee in the summer of 1862. *Egbert Benson Brown, #31447, in the collection of Wilson's Creek Battlefield. (Courtesy of the National Park Service.)*

When Coffee reached his old hometown of Greenfield around four o'clock the same afternoon, about 100 loyal citizens were at the courthouse organizing a company of Enrolled Militia under Captain Nathan McClure. The Federals had placed no pickets; so Coffee was able to ride right into town and take them by surprise. Dividing his command into two columns, he quickly surrounded the courthouse and demanded its surrender. The militia, greatly outnumbered and poorly armed, declined to make a stand.[15]

Coffee took the enrollees prisoner and ordered a guard put around them on the upper floor of the courthouse. Later, Coffee walked upstairs to address the captives, telling them that they would be treated as prisoners of war and would not be hurt. Sometime after midnight, he paroled them under the condition that they should not attempt to leave before daylight. They complied, and at dawn they

46

were allowed to retire to their homes. Coffee and his men then mounted up and headed north, taking with them all of the Union horses and arms, such as they were.[16]

When General Brown learned on August 3 of the capture of Greenfield, he armed two more companies of militia and sent them back out in pursuit of Coffee. He also sent couriers throughout the Southwest District to advise Unionists of Coffee's movements and to distribute the circular he'd issued the previous day calling for their cooperation in driving the Rebels out of the region.[17]

Brown got word two days later that Coffee had turned back after passing through Greenfield and had been spotted near Mount Vernon on the afternoon of August 4 headed south. The general fretted that the Rebels would escape the state without so much as a challenge from Federal forces. Although Coffee's raid had thus far been "singularly free from the destruction of property or life," General Brown sought to chastise the Rebels for invading his district.[18]

He needn't have worried that Coffee was fleeing for the border. The Rebel leader had no such intention. It's possible the group spotted near Mount Vernon was part of Coffee's force, but Coffee himself, after capturing Greenfield, continued northwest and went into camp on Horse Creek a few miles southeast of Montevallo with about 200 men. Recruiting over the next couple of days added at least a hundred men to this total.[19]

On the 5th of August a group of about twenty-three men were in Montevallo making preparations to join Coffee when 115 cavalrymen of the Third Wisconsin from Fort Scott rode into the village and scattered the new recruits. The Federals captured a few horses and arms and some records pertaining to Coffee's regiment.[20]

After dispersing the recruits, Colonel William Barstow, commander of the scouting expedition, turned to a group of bystanders, according to the *History of Vernon County*, and declared that he was after Colonel Coffee and that he meant to find and capture him in short order. "We will have Coffee for breakfast tomorrow morning," Barstow is reported to have boasted, "and we will take him without cream or sugar, too."[21]

The author of the county history observed with tongue in cheek, however, that "Coffee was served to the officers before they were ready for him, and he came up hot and strong, too." Some of the men who'd scattered upon Barstow's approach to Montevallo had gone straight to the main Rebel camp to report the news. Coffee promptly mounted his whole command and dashed toward the village. Warned by a Federal picket, Barstow and his command galloped south out of town on the Lamar road as Coffee entered from the east. "Col. Barstow refused his Coffee," the author of the county history concluded wryly, "and set out in a gallop for bleeding Kansas."[22]

The Rebels, numbering perhaps three or four hundred (although Union estimates suggest a larger force), charged after the fleeing Yankees, seeking to press their advantage. The outnumbered Federals kept up a running fight as they evacuated the town but were soon in full retreat, abandoning wagons and discarding sabers and other arms to lighten their loads for the race to Kansas. Coffee kept up the pursuit as far as Hogeye, about two miles beyond the Barton County line, before calling off the chase and retiring to his camp on Horse Creek.[23]

Major Benjamin S. Henning, post commander at Fort Scott, reported the next day that Barstow lost two wagons and twenty men in the Montevallo skirmish. Most of the casualties, however, were men who had been taken prisoner and who were later paroled or men who, in their aimless flight, had simply not made it back to the fort at the time of Henning's report. Among the Federals captured was Dr. Benoni Reynolds, the regimental surgeon. Coffee promptly confiscated the man's uniform and went about "sporting surgeon's straps" for the next several days."[24]

During the skirmish, the Rebels lost just one man, who was taken prisoner when the Third Wisconsin first charged into Montevallo. He was later found dead along the road out of town, apparently shot by the retreating cavalrymen when they realized they would be unable to transport him to Kansas and tend to their own safety at the same time. At least one report suggested that several of Coffee's men were also killed in the skirmishing with the Union rear guard during the pursuit, but the best evidence seems to indicate otherwise.[25]

At Montevallo, Colonel Barstow retrieved a Union revolver marked "B. Allen, Col. 16th Wis. Vol." that had been lost at the Battle of Pittsburg Landing (Shiloh) the previous spring. One Union observer took the recovered weapon as evidence of "where the troops now invading Kansas came from."[26]

On the 6th of August, the day after the Montevallo incident, a detachment of the Sixth Missouri Cavalry under the command of Major Samuel Montgomery, reinforced by about 150 militia from Polk and Cedar counties, came into the area around Horse Creek in search of Coffee. On August 7th, the Federals routed one of Coffee's camps. Montgomery reported to his superior officer, Colonel Clark Wright, that eighteen Rebels were killed, four wounded, and seventeen captured while the Federal side sustained just minor injuries.[27]

According to the *History of Vernon County*, the eighteen Missourians who died were actually killed in two separate incidents involving parties of recruits who, like those dispersed at Montevallo two days earlier, were on their way to join Coffee but that Coffee's main force was not involved in either skirmish. The county history gives convincing specifics such as the names of several of the victims and the exact location where they were buried. Montgomery conceded in his report to Clark that Coffee's command was divided between those in the Horse Creek area southeast of Montevallo and another force near Osceola, but he didn't mention the size of the group he engaged, saying only that Coffee's total force numbered about 900.[28]

By the summer of 1862, Coffee's exploits, which were no doubt exaggerated, had earned him a reputation in Union circles as an incarnate devil. On August 9, one loyalist editor reported, "Coffee's force gives no quarter to Union men, either taken in battle or at their homes; it is also reported that the women are not to be spared a fate worse than death."[29]

After overrunning the camp near Montevallo, Montgomery pressed on toward Osceola in pursuit of Coffee's main force. At Stockton, though, he inexplicably disbanded his force, allowing the militia to go home. The major then set out in pursuit of Coffee with just his one hundred regular cavalrymen, but he had second thoughts and fell back to Greenfield upon learning that Coffee was lying in ambush. An outraged General Brown ordered Montgomery placed under arrest, and he sent Colonel Wright, with 400 additional troops, to take command of Montgomery's cavalry.[30]

The arrest order was evidently rescinded, because Montgomery was soon back on Coffee's trail, chasing the Rebels to Humansville in northwest Polk County on the evening of August 11. There it was reported that Coffee had left town on the Bolivar road but had changed course toward Stockton during the night. Montgomery divided his command, dispatching the Fourth Missouri Militia (part of the troops General Brown had sent as reinforcements) in the direction of Stockton while the major and his Sixth Missouri Cavalry set out on the Bolivar road. At daylight on the 12th, the militia force came up with Coffee on the Stockton road and launched an attack. According to Montgomery's report written later the same day, the Rebels lost five men killed in the affray while the Federals had just one man wounded."[31]

During the melee, Dr. Reynolds, the surgeon who'd been captured at Montevallo, escaped by lurking in a cornfield "till the Union forces were in full command of the neighborhood." He emerged from his hiding place minus his uniform and was "cordially received" by the Union soldiers, whom he regaled with tales of "life among the butternuts."[32]

After the skirmish on the road between Humansville and Stockton, Coffee was reported "flying in the direction of Montevallo," with the Union cavalry in hot pursuit. Meanwhile, General Brown was in communication with General Blunt of the Department of Kansas, seeking assistance from Fort Scott in the hunt for Coffee. Union officials wanted to prevent a juncture with Rains, who had moved up from Arkansas through Neosho. They also sought to cut off a possible northerly movement and to trap Coffee in a deadly vise of Federal forces between Fort Scott and Springfield. They succeeded in none of the three aims. After forming a temporary junction with Rains near the Barton-Cedar county line, Coffee slipped the Federal snare and headed north toward Jackson County, where on August 16th he combined with State Guard forces under Colonels J. V. Cockrell, Upton Hays, and others to defeat 800 Federal troops at Lone Jack. According to Jackman, Coffee got lost during the maneuvering leading up to the battle, and as far as Jackman knew, took no part in the actual fighting."[33]

After the battle, Coffee and the other State Guard forces headed south for Arkansas, with troops sent out by General Blunt hounding their retreat all the way. Near Taberville in St. Clair County, at the crossing of the Osage River, a detachment of Federals under Colonel William F. Cloud caught up with the Rebels and briefly skirmished with them before being "obliged to retire." Several were wounded on each side, including Sidney Jackman of the State Guard forces. After the Federal withdrawal, the Rebels "commenced their lively skedaddle again," and Cloud resumed the pursuit, following the State Guard forces all the way to Carthage before finally abandoning the chase. Below Carthage, Colonel Wright's Sixth Missouri Cavalry took up the pursuit, aiming to drive the enemy "entirely out of the state." The Rebels were "heading for Dixie," Wright crowed. "Occasionally we catch a squad and consign them to his satanic majesty."[34]

Coffee and the other State Guard officers, though, finally eluded their pursuers and went into separate camps in extreme southwest Missouri and northwest Arkansas. Coffee quarreled with General Rains near Bentonville before crossing back into Missouri and going into camp just north of Pineville close to Upton Hays's camp. Jackman said Coffee camped in Missouri because he didn't feel at liberty to subsist his command in Arkansas, since he had thus far refused to join the Confederacy. Speaking of Coffee and Confederate colonel John C. Tracy, Jackman added, "They were independent of each other and claimed to be independent of everybody else."[35]

Around the first of September General Thomas Hindman dispatched a letter to Coffee urging him to join the Confederacy. Hindman was concerned that Coffee's undisciplined troops should be brought into regular service where they could be molded into an effective fighting force and their reckless behavior controlled. Coffee replied through another officer that he'd be glad to have his men join the Confederacy if they could do so as mounted troops. Hindman consented to the demand, although he resented Coffee's obstinacy.[36]

On September 6, Coffee and Hays skirmished with a Federal force that came down to Pineville and stole some of the grist the Rebels had been grinding at a local mill. The Federals reported killing seven Rebels, while making no mention of their own casualties.[37]

On September 9, Jo Shelby's regiment rendezvoused with Coffee and Hays at a camp between Pineville and Newtonia, and General Hindman organized the three regiments into the Missouri Cavalry Brigade under the command of Colonel Shelby. For the first time Colonel Coffee was officially a part of the Confederate Army.[38]

He did not, however, adapt easily to the demands of regular service. A little over a month later, on October 22, General Hindman arrested Coffee for drunkenness after having relieved Rains of duty the same day and for the same reason. A court martial was appointed on November 3, 1862, to hear Coffee's case, but it was dissolved eight days later, before the case came to trial. Coffee, however, was not immediately released from custody. While he was a prisoner, Hindman's army was reorganized, and Coffee's men were again placed under Shelby's command as part of the Second Brigade of General Marmaduke's Fourth Division.[29]

Marmaduke was glad to have the additional men but was unimpressed by their former leader. "Coffee's regiment numbers about 700 men," he told Hindman shortly after the reorganization. "All it wants is a good commander. Col. Coffee you know."[40]

Since Coffee had been relieved of his command because of his misconduct, he apparently did not participate in the Battle of Prairie Grove south of Fayetteville, Arkansas, on December 7, 1862. At Prairie Grove, Hindman's army was defeated by Federals under Generals James Blunt and Francis Herron. After a day-long battle with little advantage on either side, the Confederates withdrew to Van Buren near Fort Smith, leaving the Union in control of northwest Arkansas and southwest Missouri.

According to Jackman, Coffee, "with his usual vim and energy," set about recruiting a new regiment almost immediately after having been relieved of his previous command. What is known for sure is that by the beginning of 1863, he was once again wandering about in Indian Territory. Despite his concession to formality in joining the Confederacy, Coffee remained a rebel among Rebels, and he continued to operate independently much of the time. Around January 1, 1863, he and Stand Watie were driven across the Arkansas River at Fort Gibson (often called Fort Blunt) by Colonel William A. Phillips's Third Indian Home Guard. In late February or early March, Coffee was acquitted of the drunkenness charge by a Confederate court martial in Arkansas and by the end of the first week of March was once again in Missouri "on recruiting service." A Confederate report a few weeks later suggested that he would soon be officially restored to his command, but it hardly mattered, because he was already back to doing what he did best— recruiting and bushwhacking.[41]

By May, Coffee was back in the Indian Nation, where, on the 20th, he again clashed with Phillips's Indian brigade near Fort Gibson. Shortly afterwards, though, Coffee returned to Missouri, and during the summer 1863 he again kept Union officials in southwest Missouri busy chasing after him.[41]

In late May Colonel Cloud of the Second Kansas Cavalry followed Coffee north from Pineville and caught up with him, one hundred strong, at daylight on the 26th at Diamond Grove about three miles east of present-day Joplin. Cloud attacked the one hundred Rebels with a force of about equal strength and quickly dispersed them. The skirmish produced no casualties, though, because, as Cloud later complained, the Rebels "would not stand and fight but took to the woods and brush." Joel Livingston, describing the incident in his 1912 *History of Jasper County*, said, "The notable feature of this engagement was that Coffey's (sic) men fought Indian fashion, hiding in the brush and behind the big trees, thus keeping out of the way of the Kansans when they charged."[43]

Within a day or two after the skirmish at Diamond Grove, Coffee made a juncture with guerrilla leader Tom Livingston. In a classic case of the pot calling the kettle black, Livingston, in reporting the junction to General Price on May 28, referred to Colonel Coffee's men as "a small force of unorganized troops...."[44]

The combined force moved into Kansas and the Indian Nation, where the Rebels harassed Federal supply lines between Fort Scott and Fort Gibson. Coffee's union with Livingston lasted, off and on, until Livingston was killed on July 11, 1863, leading an attack on a militia company garrisoned in the Cedar County courthouse at Stockton, Missouri. Afterward, many of Livingston's men followed Coffee to Cowskin Prairie in McDonald County, where they re-organized under his command.[45]

On July 26 Brigadier General John McNeil, who had succeeded General Brown as Union commander of the District of Southwest Missouri, issued a special order directing Colonel John F. Philips of the Seventh Missouri State Militia Cavalry to operate against Coffee. Philips set out from Newtonia on the morning of the 28th headed in a southwesterly direction toward Cowskin Prairie. Union spies assured Philips that Coffee was in the area, and the scouting party found further evidence of Coffee's presence in the form of some Rebel military letters. "Additional evidence of Coffee's presence in that country," Philips reported to General McNeil "is found in the impudent and insulting conduct of the women there, who always grow most insolent and outspoken when emboldened by the presence of a rebel army."[46]

Despite Coffee's proximity, the Union expedition failed to engage the enemy, and running short on rations, Philips was, in his own words to General McNeil, "compelled to wend my way back and to lay the facts before you...." As an addendum, he included an apology for the mission's lack of success: "I exceedingly regret that we did not have a 'set-to' with Coffee. He is an old acquaintance of ours. We want to pay him back for the Lone Jack advancement."[47]

About two weeks later, Coffee, with 300 to 500 men, was still in the area of Pineville, where a small portion of his command skirmished with Federal cavalry on the 9th of August. The same day, General McNeil, apparently frustrated that his previous special orders had not eliminated Coffee's menacing presence in the district, dispatched Colonel E.C. Catherwood from the Springfield head-quarters on another special expedition against the Rebel leader.[48]

With detachments of the Sixth Missouri State Militia Cavalry, the First Arkansas Cavalry, and a section of howitzers, Catherwood set out for the southwest corner of the state. After three days' march he reached Pineville, where he met Coffee on the 13th and routed him. After receiving the colonel's dispatch from the field on August 15 proclaiming the victory, General McNeil congratulated Catherwood on his success and rejoiced that "the southwestern counties of our State are thus relieved of the terrors of a ruthless marauder and thief." Union newspapers in Missouri also saluted the news of the "ground Coffee." According to Catherwood, the Rebels lost sixty to seventy men killed, wounded, and taken prisoner in the skirmish. Coffee, however, claimed that many of the men killed were unarmed recruits, and he swore vengeance.[49]

Coffee never got the full measure of revenge he sought, but General McNeil's celebration of the Rebel leader's defeat was premature. Less than a month later, Coffee was back to his old tricks, harassing Union targets in the Southwest District. On September 6 he attacked a Federal wagon train between Fort Scott and Carthage, killing one man and capturing three. Then on September 15 he skirmished for two hours with Colonel M. La Rue Harrison in a dense grapevine thicket near Buffalo Creek in the southwest corner of Missouri before being driven south "in disorder." According to Harrison, Coffee lost at least five men killed while the Federals had no losses in either killed or wounded.[50]

Not until the fall of 1863 did the renegade Coffee, who'd supposedly been on recruiting duty throughout the summer, finally return to the fold of regular Confederate service. In early October, with 400 men, he made a juncture near Pineville with Colonel Jo Shelby, reinforcing Shelby's command for a raid that would take the Rebels all the way to the Missouri River.

After Neosho was surrendered to Shelby on October 4, Coffee killed at least two prisoners and reportedly had to be restrained by Shelby from killing all of them, approximately 180 in number, in retaliation for the affair at Pineville a month and a half earlier, because most of the captives were members of Catherwood's Sixth Missouri State Militia regiment.[51]

Shelby continued his march north and reached Coffee's hometown of Greenfield on October 6. When Coffee caught up to the advance and found the courthouse already on fire, he ordered the county records removed from the burning structure. Coffee ripped from the court records the pages pertaining to the proceedings during the current reign of provisional governor Hamilton R. Gamble, which Southerners considered a bogus administration. The rest of the records Coffee deposited in a nearby residence for safekeeping, but the effort was for naught as far as his own personal interests were concerned. After the war, he learned that the pages of the deed book containing his land records had been ripped out, just as he had ripped out the Gamble pages.[52]

Coffee's wife had died just two weeks before the Confederates reached Greenfield, and during the brief stop at his hometown, he took time to tend to the care of his five children.[53] Then Coffee and his regiment rode north out of town with the rest of Shelby's brigade.

A few days later, while Shelby was occupying Boonville, Coffee personally arrested Cooper County sheriff A.J. Barnes, who also served the county as the collector of revenue. Assuring the sheriff that he would only take public funds, Coffee relieved him of between five and six thousand dollars in county money. However, he also took another three thousand that Barnes had collected for various executions and that he claimed was his own private money.[54]

When Shelby's brigade retuned to Arkansas in the fall of 1863, Marmaduke once again balked at accepting Coffee into his command, and he expressed the opinion that there was "some illegality in the organization of Coffee's regiment." Colonel Robert C. Newton, General Hindman's assistant adjutant general, directed

Marmaduke to state the facts formally or "the organization will otherwise be legal."[55]

Whether Marmaduke ever stated his objection formally is not known, but in the spring of 1864, Coffee again left his regiment or was relieved of duty. Then the following summer, during the reorganization of Price's army for the raid into Missouri, Coffee was given command of a "paper" regiment in Jackman's brigade of Shelby's division. Coffee was expected to fill out the regiment with new recruits, and when he had still not completed the task two weeks into the 1864 raid, Shelby ordered him to report to General Price, who reassigned Coffee's ragtag outfit to Charles Tyler's brigade of the same division.[56]

In late 1864 or early 1865, after Price's raid had ended in humiliating defeat, Coffee moved his family to Waco, Texas. He then returned to northern Arkansas, where his regiment annoyed Union officials by cutting telegraph wires and committing other depredations throughout the spring. Toward the end of the war General Shelby reportedly asked Coffee to join his expedition into Mexico, but Coffee declined. Instead he turned himself in at Jacksonport, Arkansas, still holding the same rank of colonel he had at the start of the war. According to Jackman, Coffee could have been a major general, but, because of the "demon whiskey," he never fulfilled his potential as a military officer. Coffee was released on June 5, 1865, but his actual parole and his signing of an oath of allegiance to the United States was not officially executed until July 26, 1865, at Austin, Texas. After the war, Coffee remained in Texas and died at Brownsville in 1890.[57]

6
Tom Livingston and the
Burning of Sherwood

Before the Civil War, Thomas R. Livingston ran a general store and owned a lead smelter with his half-brother, William Parkinson, at French Point, Missouri. This was a small settlement on Center Creek in Jasper County about two miles west of Minersville (present-day Oronogo). Although Livingston had a reputation for whiskey drinking and fist-fighting in the mining camps around Jasper County, he was considered a prominent citizen in the area. The thirty-nine-year-old widower and father of two was described by one observer as "a big, square shouldered man whose weight might have been in the neighborhood of 175 pounds" and who, at least before the war, "was always clean shaven except for his moustache."[1]

When the Civil War came on, Livingston helped Sanford J. Talbott raise a regiment in the Jasper County area for the Missouri State Guard. The regiment was assigned to the Eighth Division and designated the Eleventh Cavalry, with Livingston second in command to Colonel Talbott. As a member of the State Guard, Livingston presumably participated in early actions of the Trans-Mississippi war like the engagement at Carthage and the Battle of Wilson's Creek. In early September, Livingston accompanied John Matthews, leader of a ragtag band of guerrillas and Confederate Indians, on a raid of Humboldt, Kansas. Upon their arrival, the Rebels announced that they had come after John Gilmore, a former partner of Livingston, against whom he held a grudge. The raiders captured Gilmore, confiscated his stock of goods, and plundered the town.[2]

Then, in mid-October, as part of Colonel Talbott's command, Livingston helped carry out a second raid on Humboldt. On the evening of the 13th, approximately 300 men under Talbott left Preston in northern Jasper County, not far from Livingston's home at French Point, and marched toward Humboldt. Reaching the town the following evening, they swept in and took possession of the place. After putting the men of the village under guard, the Missourians burned the town in retaliation, they said, for the sacking of Osceola by Kansas senator Jim Lane and his jayhawkers three weeks earlier.[3]

Realizing resistance was futile, a local doctor invited the Rebel leaders to take supper with him, and Tom Livingston was one of those who reportedly took him up on the offer. After the raid, the Missouri troops headed back to Missouri in the direction of Sherwood, a small town in the western part of Jasper County not far from Livingston's home at French Point.[4]

When the term of enlistment for the Missouri State Guard troops expired in February of 1862, about half of the Eleventh Cavalry entered regular Confederate service, but the other half returned to Jasper County, where they hoped to retire to relatively peaceful lives.[5]

It was not to be. By the beginning of 1862, the South's prospect of holding Missouri was growing bleak, and the Confederate effort in the state was turning increasingly into a vicious, irregular warfare that often pitted neighbor against neighbor. Partisan bands roved the countryside bent on destroying Union targets, tormenting loyal citizens, and harassing the invading Federal army. It was hard for anyone to stay neutral.

Many of the State Guard cavalrymen who returned to Jasper County soon joined Livingston, who was mustering an irregular force in the area.[6]

Sometime in early 1862, Livingston took his men and enlisted in the Provisional Army of the Confederate States, and they were assigned to the Confederate Indian Brigade under Brigadier General Albert Pike. Officially designated the First Missouri Battalion, Livingston's command was attached to Colonel Stand Watie's Cherokee regiment and was sometimes called the Cherokee Rangers or other, more colorful, names like the Bloody Spikes. Livingston was given the rank of major, but despite the loose Confederate affiliation, his command continued to operate as a roving, independent band most of the time.[7]

Livingston's men, like most guerrillas in the state, were superbly mounted and armed to the hilt, with as many as three or four Colt revolvers thrust into their belts and one or two other weapons carried in saddle holsters or strapped to their backs. They usually wore ordinary civilian clothing, although some occasionally donned Federal uniforms stolen from the enemy.[8] Livingston himself was said to have sometimes worn a broad-brimmed, white hat, making him a striking figure but also a convenient target.[9]

About the time Livingston joined Pike's Indian Brigade, he accompanied the command to Mount Vernon, where it was temporarily stationed in early February 1862.[10] While lingering in Lawrence County, Livingston and his men went out on a foraging expedition in the Verona area, raided a home, and took three occupants prisoner. They strung one of the captives up to an apple tree before letting him down alive. Then, according to the 1888 *History of Lawrence County*, all three "were tied in a bunch and made to travel in that form half way to Mt. Vernon." The next day the unfettered but still closely guarded prisoners were herded to a farm east of Mount Vernon, where they "were given the work of killing hogs."[11]

About the same time and in the same county, Livingston reportedly made a speech that startled many of his listeners because of its pro-Union slant.[12] Presumably he lashed out at the Confederacy for its indifferent defense of Missouri.

During the spring of 1862, Livingston roamed the "neutral lands" of southeast Kansas (present-day Cherokee and Crawford counties), where he and other officers of Pike's command, "with their barbarous gangs of Indians and scarcely less inhuman whites," found diversion harassing squatters and driving them from the area.[13]

On May 29, Livingston's "scouts" provided Colonel Stand Watie with intelligence of a Federal camp near Neosho in southwest Missouri, and two days later Stand Watie combined with Missouri State Guard colonel John T. Coffee to attack and rout the Federals. In his report of the affair the next day, Stand Waite credited "Captain Livingston" for informing him of the Federals' location.[14]

Although the irregular partisan bands served a useful role in the Southern effort and their marauding activities received tacit approval if not official sanction, not all regular Confederate officers looked upon them with favor. Livingston's band was no exception. In July, the guerrillas roamed into Indian Territory, where Livingston and Colonel Coffee's indiscriminate activities provoked the censure of General Pike. Another Confederate officer later admitted that some of Livingston's men were "no better than thieves and robbers."[15]

Livingston didn't stray for long in Indian Territory before returning to southwest Missouri. In an August 9, 1862 report Union brigadier general Frederick Salomon, who had just completed a march from Sarcoxie to a camp near Fort Scott, complained to General Blunt, Commander of the District of Kansas, that "Neosho was occupied by the enemy under Jackman and Livingston, on August 6" and that "great rejoicing had been among the secesh population there, dinners prepared for them, etc." Later in the report Salomon groused that "...all Southwestern Missouri is evacuated by Union troops and occupied by a five-times stronger rebel force than all available troops under my command."[16]

In mid-August 1862 Tom Livingston's guerrillas skirmished with some of Colonel Cloud's Second Kansas Cavalry at Pilot Grove near the northeast edge of present-day Joplin. The following day, a company of Cloud's command under Captain Harris S. Greeno discovered part of a large Confederate force in northern Jasper County under Captain Jo Shelby, who was resting on Coon Creek after a recruiting trip into northern Missouri. Mistaking the Rebels for Livingston's men, Greeno charged into the brush after them and was routed as a result. The Federal loss was five killed and eleven wounded, including Greeno himself.[17]

In late September of 1862, Livingston's band and some of Stand Watie's Indians fell in with Colonel T.C. Hawpe's Thirty-first Texas Cavalry and scouted through Jasper County. On September 20, the combined Rebel force came upon and attacked the Federal Second Indian Home Guard (Kansas) under Colonel John Ritchie, who was camped on Spring River in northwest Jasper County at what was known as Shirley Ford (named after the family of Myra Maybelle Shirley—a.k.a. Belle Starr—whose family had settled in the area during Jasper County's early days.). Many in the Federal Indian regiment had brought their families with them on the jaunt into Missouri, and when the Rebels fired upon the Federal picket around eight o'clock in the morning, according to Ritchie, "...a regular stampede of about 1,500 women and children crowded into camp for protection, making a regular Bull Run retreat."[18]

Ritchie, however, managed to rally his troops and repel the assault, then later in the day mounted a charge of his own. In describing the enemy retreat, Ritchie boasted that "such another skedaddling could not have been beaten, only by the women and children in the morning, and that only because they were more in number." He went on to admit, however, that the number of casualties during the engagement was similar on each side—about twenty dead. Another Union report claimed that some of the Cherokee Indians among the Rebels "indulged in the pastime of scalping" several of the dead Federals.[19]

After Ritchie's initial retreat, the Federal Indians took up defensive positions in some heavy brush, and the Confederates launched several assaults trying to dislodge them but were unable to penetrate the thick scrub on horseback. According to the *History of Jasper County*, Livingston finally proposed to the Texas commander that, instead of attacking the enemy head-on, they should charge down the main road and cut the Federals off from their wagon train, which had already forded the river. "Colonel, if you will give me command of your regiment for thirty minutes," Livingston is supposed to have said, "I will capture the whole damn regiment, wagon train and all."[20]

When the Texas commander rejected the idea, an argument between the two leaders ensued, and the colonel ordered Livingston and his men to the rear.

"Colonel," the hot-blooded Livingston retorted, "you can take your regiment and go straight to hell and I will take my command and go where I damn please."

Without another word, the Texan turned his command to the north and rode off the battlefield. Livingston waited until the Texans were out of sight, then rode in the opposite direction, leaving the Indians in possession of the field.

Less than a week later, Union patrols spotted Livingston in Kansas. On September 26, Colonel William Weer of the Kansas Second Brigade, citing intelligence from two scouting parties, informed General Salomon that Livingston and Colonel Stand Watie were in the vicinity of Baxter Springs, and Weer fretted that Confederate forces in the region were amassing for an attack against him at his camp on Jenkins Creek in eastern Jasper County.[21]

On October 15 Livingston was reported on the Dry Fork of Spring River north of Carthage lying in ambush with 200 men for a Union wagon train which was scheduled to pass the location under the escort of Union Captain George F. Earl. The post Commander at Fort Scott, Major B.S. Henning of the Third Wisconsin Cavalry, immediately sent Captain Theodore Conkey to reinforce Earl at Carthage, and although Livingston was found to be lying in wait as reported, he declined to launch an attack and let the train pass safely through to Fort Scott.[22]

About this same time Livingston captured a couple of loyal citizens in an attempt to ransom the freedom of several guerrillas being held at Fort Scott. He and Major Henning entered into a negotiation for an exchange of prisoners, with Henry Taylor of Vernon County acting as an intermediary, and three guerrillas, including John Bishop, were released.[23]

In early November, Livingston came across a Union wagon train that was returning from General Blunt's army in northwest Arkansas to Fort Scott for supplies. The guerrillas trailed the train, consisting of about a hundred wagons, for three or four days and made several attempts to capture it, killing three soldiers of the guard during the various skirmishes. The Rebels followed the train to within eight miles of Fort Scott on November 7 before retiring to a less taxing endeavor. Withdrawing to western Vernon County, they killed at least two Union men, wounded several others, and took eight or ten prisoners. One of the victims, a man named Howard, was supposedly "shot in cold blood after he had surrendered himself up to them." A messenger sent to Fort Scott with news of the raid reached the installation on the 7th, just a few hours after the Federal wagon train, and reported that Livingston was in Vernon County on Dry Wood Creek with a hundred men, "murdering and robbing" citizens of the area and "working upstream."[24]

Henning immediately sent Captain David Mefford with seventy-five men to intercept the guerrillas. The Union company struck Livingston's trail at Cato just across the border in Crawford County, Kansas, "pursued him about twenty-five miles to Cow Creek, and overtook him, making a running fight, and wounding one of Livingston's men and recovering some prisoners."[25]

Because his horses were exhausted, Mefford was forced to break off the pursuit and return to Fort Scott, but in the meantime Henning had sent word to Captain Conkey and Captain C.F. Coleman, whom he'd earlier dispatched to Lamar (in response to Quantrill's attack there), to change course and intercept Livingston at Sherwood. Conkey and Coleman took up the chase and camped the night of the 8th on Spring River above Sherwood. The next morning, "The command then separated, Captain Coleman on the south side of Spring River and Captain Conkey on the north side, and worked down toward Sherwood, and Captain Coleman being in the advance came upon the enemy and charged them, killing four or five and taking four prisoners, including the notorious Captain Baker, who was taken by Captain Coleman himself." This was a reference to Moses Baker, a captain in Livingston's command and a prominent landowner in western Jasper County before the war.[26]

A civilian eyewitness to this skirmish, George B. Walker, recalled years later that each side captured about an equal number of prisoners and that Livingston and Conkey, with a Southern girl acting as a go-between, entered into a negotiation for their exchange. According to Walker, Livingston "insisted that in trading prisoners Conkey throw in a gallon of whisky 'to boot.'" After the captain consented to this and delivered the liquor, the guerrilla leader demanded that a Union soldier sample the drink to show it wasn't tainted. "This was done," Walker remembered, "and when the trade was completed, Livingston and his men consumed the whisky and pronounced it good."[27]

Shortly after this episode, Livingston drifted south in search of winter quarters. A Union report on Christmas morning of 1862 placed him in the area of Fort Gibson in Indian Territory.[28]

Around the 10th of January, 1863, he skirmished with a company of Colonel William A. Phillips's Third Indian Home Guard in Indian Territory about thirty-five miles from Elm Springs, Arkansas. Livingston and his command of about sixty or seventy men "were preparing winter quarters" when their camp was discovered. According to Phillips, the guerrillas "drew up in the woods and offered sharp resistance, which lasted about fifteen minutes, and the enemy fled, leaving several dead and a number taken prisoners." Phillips said the Federals lost but one man dead.[29]

Just a few days later, Livingston had another "spirited little affair" with some of Phillips's men near Maysville. According to Phillips, when the Union force advanced on the enemy in three separate columns, the guerrillas broke and "...ran from the first into the second, and finally into the third. Not less than 25 or 30 Rebels must have been killed or disabled.[30]

Livingston had yet another skirmish with Federal troops in the area just a day or so later. Around January 15, Major A.C. Ellithorpe, commanding 500 mounted men on a march from Elm

Springs, "surprised a party of Livingston's gang" and "...killed nine and captured thirteen of the gentry."[31]

His repeated run-ins with Union forces in the area may have inspired Livingston to abort his southern stay and reclaim the friendlier territory of his home grounds. In any case, his winter visit to Arkansas and Indian Territory proved brief. By February 11 he was back in Missouri, where he was "getting troublesome" in the Neosho area, according to Colonel Phillips.[32]

Livingston and his band of sixty men continued to move north to the area of Dry Fork. On February 19, from "Camp Crouch" several miles north of Carthage, the Rebel chief issued a parole to a Union man named William H. Atkinson whom the guerrillas had taken prisoner. It read as follows:

> Know all men by these presents, that I, the undersigned do solemnly sware before boath God and man, and pledge my life, property and sacred honor that I will return to my home (Fort Scott, Kansas), as a peaceable and neutral citizen in the present war and difficulty now existing between the United States so-called and the Confederate States of America, that I will not aid nor assist in any way or manner whatsoever in the present difficulty between the two governments, so help me God.
> W.H.A.
> Witness—Capt. A.S. Humbard.
> Sworn to and subscribed before me this, the 19th day of February, 1863.
> T.R. Livingston,
> Maj. Com'g 1st Battalion Cherokee Spikes

"His (Livingston's) orthography is not always according to Webster," a Union observer remarked wryly, "but this is not essential to bushwhacking against the 'so-called' U.S."[33]

The same day and in the same area, Livingston, commanding sixty men, skirmished with a company of Enrolled Missouri Militia from Bower's Mill. Major Edward B. Eno of the Eighth Missouri State Militia Cavalry headquartered at Newtonia was camped at Carthage that same evening and filed a report three days later describing the action. With more than a dash of sarcasm Eno noted that, after fighting with Livingston "a little," the enrolled militia "came charging back through Carthage, swearing because they could not catch him."[34]

The Enrolled Missouri Militia was a Federal home guard force organized in August of 1862, which was called into service from time to time to repel a particular threat or when other circumstances warranted. All able-bodied men were expected to enlist, and, although most enrollees were staunch Unionists (because the majority of Southern sympathizers had already joined the Confederacy or taken to the bush), the conscription of such citizen soldiers produced many reluctant warriors like those from Bower's Mill. Often they were friends and neighbors of the guerrillas they were expected to eradicate and sometimes secretly sympathized with the enemy.

After his skirmish with the Enrolled Missouri Militia, Livingston ranged north toward Lamar, and Eno chose not to pursue him, because he felt the guerrilla band would encounter the Wisconsin Volunteer Cavalry operating in the that area. Livingston did run into troops sent out from Fort Scott, but not the Wisconsin Cavalry. Instead, he had a scrape with Captain Coleman and a detachment of the Ninth Kansas Cavalry. Coleman succeeded in driving off the guerrillas but lost several men in the process.[35]

Meanwhile, Eno marched below Carthage to scour the thickets around Jones and Jenkins creeks in southeastern Jasper County. Another dose of his sardonic wit clearly shows the secessionist sentiment that predominated in the area. "We took the brush and creek until within a quarter of a mile of that misnomer, Fidelity;" he remarked dryly, "then charged into that place; came upon a small party of the rascals, wounded one and captured three. The balance escaped, our horses being too tired to overtake them."[36] Eno didn't disclose the disposition of the captured infidels.

In his report, he instead turned his attention back to Livingston. "If the Wisconsin scout does not come across Livingston and cut him up, he will go down to the border and harbor at the mouth of Shoal creek again, provided he does not leave the country altogether." Eno then expanded on the latter prospect by asserting that even many of Livingston's best friends were beginning to recognize the damage the guerrillas were doing in the area and were considering presenting the guerrilla chief with a petition to leave.[37]

Eno's intelligence that Livingston might soon leave the area proved to be a bit of wishful thinking. About two weeks later, on the night of March 3, 1863, Livingston and a hundred men charged into Granby where twenty-five of Eno's battalion were stationed. Two men on guard duty were captured and presumed shot to death as nothing was later heard from them. "Two other soldiers," according to Eno, "who were attending a sick family a short distance outside the stockade were captured, and unarmed as they were, begging for their lives, were shot down in their tracks." Livingston then turned and galloped quickly out of town without risking an assault on the stockade.[38]

Union forces clashed with Livingston again less than a week later in western Jasper County. Captain Mefford, with three companies of the Sixth Kansas Cavalry, camped the night of March 8 at Sherwood after a scout through the county along Turkey Creek. Early the next morning, following up a trail located the evening before, Mefford's advance ran into a Rebel picket, and shots were fired. According to Mefford, he then "searched the woods and found the camp, which had contained about 70 or 80 men, judging from appearances, which the noted Tom Livingston had left in great haste, cutting halters and ropes...."[39]

Mefford was unable to pursue the guerrillas because of the thick brush but instead moved out onto the prairie at the edge of Turkey Creek and marched about two miles before spotting several men at a stand of timber near the northwestern edge of present-day Joplin. Mefford's advance chased the men about three-quarters of a mile before "they were suddenly turned upon by Livingston's whole force and obliged to fall back to the main command, still pursued."[40]

Seeing his advance repelled, Mefford formed his men behind a stand of trees and brush, dismounted them, and sent them into the timber on foot. Livingston charged to within ninety or a hundred yards of the brake and exchanged fire with the cavalrymen for several minutes before retreating rapidly. Mefford reported only one man injured. Livingston's losses were unknown, "but, from the appearance of the woods, must have been considerable in horses." Joel Livingston's *History of Jasper County* says, "The Confederate scouts sustained a severe loss."[41]

Around mid-March, 1863, Livingston and Major Henning entered into negotiations again involving the exchange of prisoners and other matters. Henning sent Livingston a note on March 12 proposing an exchange, and Livingston replied on March 17 from his camp at Brush Creek pressing the terms of the agreement. Livingston demanded the release of J.W. Bryson, "a private belonging to my command, who is confined in Springfield Prison.

You will likewise release J.G. Haslet, who is in prison at Fort Lincoln." Livingston was particularly concerned that Captain Baker, the man whom Captain Coleman of Henning's command had captured the previous fall near Sherwood, should be released. Henning had previously suggested that Baker might be released, but Livingston had heard nothing of him. "It looks hard," Livingston said, "for you to hold him a prisoner so long as you have held him after the liberality that I have shown you and your men. As I am sure there can be no just charges against Capt. Baker that he should be in prison for and further there is no officer in either army that has acted more honorable to the opposite party than Capt. Baker has. Yet it seems that you still hold him."[42]

Henning obviously did not share Livingston's high opinion of Captain Baker, because Baker had already been executed. Known in Union circles as a "notorious character on Shoal Creek and Spring River," Baker had reportedly attended the hanging of a Union man named John Ireland in September of 1861, and he was accused of being the one who had placed the rope around Ireland's neck. (The hanging was in retaliation for the death of a Southern sympathizer in August of 1861.) Thus, shortly after having been lodged in jail at Fort Scott, Baker had been sent out on an "errand" to fetch water and had been shot and killed by his guard."[43]

Livingston continued his letter to Henning by citing a compromise that the two parties had tentatively fashioned. The pact apparently involved an agreement that each side would be entitled to forage unmolested in certain specified territory. "I am under the impression," Livingston added, "if Gen. Cloud, you, and myself could meet, that we could easily come to an understanding, as from what I have heard of both of you, there is very little difference in our views in regard to the present difficulty. I am contending for the old constitution in every particular and down on the Abolitionist Doctrine."[44]

Livingston concluded the note by appending a long list of Federal soldiers that he had paroled without an exchange. He signed the letter, "T.R. Livingston, Major, Commanding 1st Battalion Cherokee Spikes." Then, leaving Captain Andrew J. Pearcy in charge of his band in the Jasper County area, Livingston started the next day toward the headquarters of General Douglas Cooper, who'd succeeded General Pike in command of the Indian brigade, to bring up the balance of his men.[45]

By the spring of 1863 Tom Livingston had become such a vexation to Union leaders in the region that they sometimes falsely sighted him or exaggerated his force. On April 1, Colonel M. La Rue Harrison of the First Arkansas Cavalry reported to General Samuel R. Curtis that Livingston was in southwestern Missouri "with 800 guerrillas."[46] Despite the date of the correspondence, Harrison's alarm suggests that Livingston had ceased to be an April Fool's joke to Union officials. It hardly mattered that Livingston was, in reality, somewhere off in Indian Territory leading a mere handful of Rebels.

Despite Livingston's temporary absence from the Jasper County area, Union officials were still busy dealing with the menacing threat he presented. When Major Charles W. Blair replaced Major Henning as post commander at Fort Scott in the spring of 1863, one of his main charges was the task of quashing the noted guerrilla leader. To the same end, troops from the First Kansas Colored Infantry Regiment were stationed at an outpost at Baxter Springs under Colonel James M. Williams.

This was the same unit of black troops that had skirmished the previous October with guerrillas at Island Mound in Bates County and had, according to one Federal officer, heroically answered the often-posed question of whether they would fight.[47] Confederate sympathizers, of course, deeply resented the enlistment of blacks into the Federal army, and partisans in the Jasper County area especially resented the presence at nearby Baxter Springs of Williams's troops, some of whom were ex-slaves from southwest Missouri.

On May 5 Major Blair sent a detachment from Fort Scott to attack a guerrilla camp that he'd learned was established on Center Creek near Sherwood. Reinforced by two companies from the newly organized regiment at Baxter Springs, the Union force "attacked the enemy at daybreak, carrying the camp in gallant style and dispersing the Rebels in every direction." The scouting party subsequently broke up another camp in the same area, then headed back to Kansas with several captured prisoners and about fifty confiscated horses and mules. The Union press reported that, although the troops did not succeed in finding Livingston, they "got up a big scare among the rebs."[48]

The reason the Federals failed to find Livingston was that the Center Creek camps were not his. Instead, they were likely those of Charles Harrison, a former lieutenant colonel in Emmett

MacDonald's Missouri cavalry regiment, who had recently appeared in the Jasper County area and, according to one Union report, taken charge of "all the squads, hands and gangs abroad in the country, outranking Tom R. Livingston, who is still absent...." Harrison, though, was just passing through and stayed only long enough to enlist a few reinforcements for the mission he was about to undertake. Just a few days after the Union attack on the Sherwood camps, Harrison headed across Kansas in command of a corps of officers who were on their way to Colorado and New Mexico to recruit and organize for the Confederate Army. On May 15, near the Verdigris River southwest of Humboldt, Harrison's party of nineteen men was attacked and virtually annihilated by a band of Union-allied Osage Indians under Chief Little Bear. The Osages killed all but two of the Rebels, "scalped and cut off the heads of their victims, and stripped them of all valuables and clothing." The warriors then reportedly "held a big war dance over the trophies."[49]

Livingston himself was still resting in Indian Territory at the time of the May 5 attack on the Center Creek camps. According to his own report of May 28, 1863, to General Sterling Price, Livingston left the Creek Agency on the 6th of May headed for Missouri. On the 8th he skirmished at Cabin Creek with a scouting party from Fort Scott, "killing one and wounding one" of the enemy. The Federal detachment then took shelter in and around some nearby houses, and Livingston tried unsuccessfully to draw them out before retiring as Union reinforcements approached. Livingston put his own loss at three men slightly injured.[50]

The Union version is somewhat different. Colonel Phillips, commander of Fort Blunt in the Indian Nation, said that, after fighting with Livingston's men for about an hour, the Union party, which was on its way to the fort with the mail, "routed them, killing three and wounding several."[51]

While Livingston was absent from Southwest Missouri, Southern sympathizers in the area boasted that he would "sweep over this district like a tornado" when he returned. When the guerrilla chief arrived back in the state on May 9, both sides took up the challenge. Around this date, Livingston's men raided into southeast Kansas and, according to a Union report, "committed murders and robberies which always accompany a guerrilla invasion." In response, Colonel Thomas T. Crittenden, post commander at Newtonia, sent Major Eno on a scout into Jasper County in search of his old adversary on May 13.[52]

Eno, in command of one hundred men from his own Eighth Missouri State Militia Cavalry and another eighty-four from the Seventh Missouri State Militia Cavalry proceeded north to Shoal Creek, where Captain Squire Ballew of the Seventh was sent west with orders to scout along the creek, then turn north and rendezvous with Eno the next day at French Point, Livingston's old stomping grounds. Major Eno and the rest of the command camped that evening on Center Creek five miles from Carthage.[53]

The next morning Eno again divided his command, sending Captain Jacob Cassairt of the Eighth Missouri State Militia Cavalry with forty men and Captain Murline C. Henslee of the Seventh with thirty-five men down either side of Center Creek toward French Point while Eno and the remainder of the command followed in the middle along the banks of the creek. About 3:00 p.m. approximately a mile and a half east of French Point, Cassairt and Henslee drove in Livingston's pickets and converged on the south side of the creek, where, according to Eno, they encountered the main guerrilla force, "about 100 strong...posted under cover of a log house and dense brush. A severe fight ensued of some fifteen minutes' duration, when our men were obliged to fall back."[54]

Eno blamed the retreat on the fact that Henslee's horse became unmanageable and carried the captain away from his men and the fact that many of Livingston's men were wearing Federal uniforms. Cassairt's detachment mistook the blue-clad guerrillas for Union soldiers and "before discovering their mistake were right among them, had received a galling fire, and were fighting hand-to-hand."[55]

Eno himself was two miles up the creek when the firing commenced, and although he immediately galloped toward the sound of the shooting, he "was not able to reach the ground until all was over." He pressed on after Livingston, hoping to drive the guerrillas into Captain Ballew's detachment moving upstream, but when he reached French Point, he learned to his exasperation that Ballew had merely fired a few times at Livingston's advance and then retreated, allowing the guerrillas to escape.[56]

The partisans broke into small groups, and Eno pursued them over the next four days "almost continually fighting them, starting up scattered squads of from four to ten, chasing and firing on them, when they invariably dashed into the brush and concealed themselves...."[57]

Colonel Crittenden put a slightly better face on the behavior of his men than Eno. He stated in his report of the affray that the scouting party completely routed Livingston, and he made no mention of the initial Federal retreat or of Ballew's dubious effort. Both officers agreed, however, that Rebel casualties greatly outnumbered their own—about fifteen guerrillas killed compared to only four Union soldiers. Crittenden concluded by saying of the guerrillas, "A quick succession of vigorous scouts will destroy and disperse them. Kill Livingston, and there is no one else to mass and congregate these bands. Is a man of much influence."[58]

The Confederate side of the story is predictably quite different in the number of casualties and other details. In his report of May 28, Livingston said that on the 15th (Eno said the 14th), "as I was crossing the timber of Centre Creek, about 10 miles southwest of Carthage, I encountered a scout of the enemy, consisting of 125 Newtonia militia. I immediately got my men in position to receive an assault from him, whom I vigorously repulsed." Livingston then charged and "A sharp firing ensued; the enemy were soon flying before us, being completely put to rout. I pursued him about three miles." The guerrilla chief estimated Union losses at thirteen killed and four mortally wounded and claimed his own loss was just two men slightly injured.[59]

On the 18th of May, Eno gave up his chase after Livingston and went back to Newtonia, allowing the guerrillas to turn their attention to more agreeable pursuits. When Livingston's scouts reported sixty soldiers and a mule train from Colonel Williams's Negro regiment foraging on the Center Creek prairie near Sherwood that very day, Livingston saw a rare opportunity for vengeance on the hated black troops.

He promptly led sixty-seven of his "best mounted men" toward the scene and came upon the Federals at the home of a Mrs. Rader. The foraging party was led by Major Richard G. Ward, the same officer who had commanded the black troops in Bates County the previous fall, and his party numbered, according to Union reports, from twenty-five to thirty-two Negro soldiers and from twenty to twenty-two white artillery men from the Second Kansas Battery. The Federals had driven the woman, whose son was one of Livingston's guerrillas, from her house and were busy pillaging the premises. About twenty of the black troops had stacked their arms in the yard and were in the home rummaging for provisions, with some of them upstairs tossing corn into the wagons below.[60]

"I charged them at the house," said Livingston in his May 28 report, "flanking them on the right, routed them, and pursued them about 8 miles, to the crossing of Spring River."[61]

Many of Colonel Williams's black soldiers, on foot and unarmed, were shot before they could flee or reach their weapons. The pursuit mentioned by Livingston involved mainly the mounted troops. These were the white officers and a few artillery men from the Second Kansas Battery who'd come along on the expedition. During the chase, three men from the battery were killed and two captured. A third white soldier and two of Williams's black soldiers were also captured.[62]

Livingston put the enemy loss at "negroes, 23, and 7 white men" while his own command "sustained no loss." The guerrillas also captured the mule train and a good deal of guns and ammunition.[63]

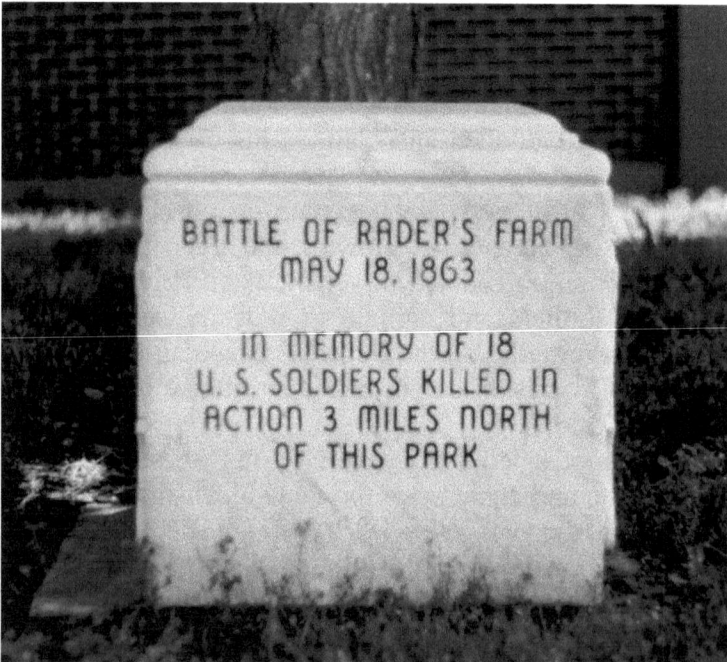

Monument at the Joplin Museum Complex to soldiers killed at Rader's farm.

The next day after the guerrillas' attack on the foraging party, Union troops from Kansas came back, 300 strong according to Livingston's report, and burned the town of Sherwood and eleven farm houses in the area. "They put 10 of their dead (negroes) that had been left on the battle-ground the day preceding, and, together with the body of Mr. John Bishop, a citizen prisoner, whom they had murdered, into the house of Mrs. Rador, and burned the premises. They then returned to their camp at Baxter Springs."[64]

Bishop was, in fact, more than a "citizen" prisoner. He was the same man who had been released by Major Henning in the prisoner exchange with Livingston the previous fall. When the soldiers came upon him near the Rader place tending the Federal mules that the guerrillas had captured during their attack the previous day, Bishop was taken to the house and executed for violating his parole. Livingston's account of the events surrounding the burning of Sherwood is otherwise essentially confirmed in a letter one of the Union participants wrote to his wife three days after the destruction.[65]

Many of the citizens who had their homes burned fled to Texas, and although some returned after the war, the town, which had been Jasper County's third largest, was never rebuilt.

On May 20, the day after the burning of Sherwood, Livingston and Williams entered into negotiations for an exchange of prisoners. Writing from "Camp Jackson," Livingston proposed trading the three white soldiers he'd captured two days earlier for any Confederate soldiers Williams might be holding. "As for the negroes," Livingston said, "I cannot recognize them as soldiers, and in consequence, I will have to hold them as contraband of war."[66]

Williams responded the next day accepting Livingston's proposal for an exchange of the white prisoners. In answer to Livingston's veiled threat to kill the two prisoners from the colored regiment, however, Williams said he was holding back a similar number of Confederate captives and promised to "follow suit or trump" if Livingston carried through with the threat.[67]

Livingston wrote back on May 23 threatening to kill three Federals for every Confederate captive executed by Colonel Williams. The missive was signed, "T. R. Livingston, Major Commanding 1st Battalion Bloody Spikes."[68]

About this time, one of the black prisoners was killed in the guerrilla camp, and the strained negotiations took on an even nastier tone. Livingston claimed a visitor to camp, over whom the guerrilla chief had no authority, shot the prisoner during an altercation between the two men, but Williams was unconvinced. He told Livingston in a May 26 correspondence that if the guilty party was not delivered to the Federal camp within forty-eight hours, he'd hang a Confederate prisoner.[69]

Livingston replied the next day from his camp at Diamond Grove, Missouri, that he could not comply with the demand and pointed out that the prisoners being held by Williams did not belong to the guerrilla command. "Consequently," Livingston concluded, "the innocent will have to suffer for the guilty."[70]

Negotiations broke off after this, and each side started killing prisoners.[71]

Toward the end of May, John T. Coffee came up from Pineville to join Livingston, "making a force of 800 to 1,000," according to General Blunt's estimate. The combined Rebel force roamed into Kansas and Indian Territory, threatening Williams's black regiment at Baxter Springs, harassing Colonel Phillips's Indian brigade, and disrupting the lines of supply and communication between Fort Scott and Fort Gibson.[72]

On June 8, while most of the Federals from Baxter Springs were out on a scout for Livingston, the Rebel chieftain dashed toward the Union camp they'd just left and attacked a small party of soldiers from the Second Kansas Battery who were tending a herd of horses nearby. The guerrillas killed one man, took two prisoners, and also captured the horses. Shortly afterward, Livingston and Colonel Williams tried briefly to negotiate another prisoner exchange, but the incident at the Rader farm and its aftermath had soured whatever good faith had previously existed. The bargaining yielded no agreement, and Livingston promptly killed the two captives.[73]

Returning to Missouri, the guerrillas carried out a raid on the small settlement of Blytheville, a precursor to the town of Joplin. Then around the middle of June, about the same time that Williams's black regiment marched south into Indian Territory, Livingston moved off to the north. He and Coffee, according to Union colonel John Edwards's report of the 19th, passed Carthage with about 300 men, a more creditable estimate than Blunt's extravagant calculation three weeks earlier.[74]

This northward movement during the middle of June is consistent with a report that reached Jefferson City shortly after the burning of Butler on the night of June 21 that the guerrillas who carried out the raid were "part of Livingston's gang," but the report is unconfirmed by other sources.[75]

Livingston met his end three weeks later leading an assault on a Union detachment at Stockton in Cedar County. On Saturday, July 11, 1863, at about 1:00 p.m., according to the report of Major Charles Sheppard filed four days later, "Livingston, the chief of bushwhackers in this district, with 100 men, surprised and attacked..." a small detachment of militiamen garrisoned in the courthouse. A number of soldiers, who were outside the courthouse lounging on the grounds of the square listening to a political speech in the noonday heat, dispersed at the first sign of the Rebels, leaving only about twenty men inside the building to defend the courthouse. These few, however, quickly rallied, barricaded the building, and returned fire.[76]

W.R. Willett, one of the militiamen inside the courthouse, recounted the episode years later. Livingston, he said, "armed with a heavy, breech-loading pistol to which he had attached a rifle stock...," galloped into town and "rode at top speed up to the court house, reined in his horse and fired into the building just as we swung the heavy door into place." During the brief but heated exchange that followed, Livingston "was shot from his horse close to the building as he urged his men on to the attack."[77]

As his men retreated, Livingston tried to rise, but several of the Unionists dashed from the courthouse to stop him. One, "who had picked up the fallen man's gun, dealt him a terrific blow on the head, and at the same time several others fired into his body."[78]

Sheppard reported the Union loss at four mortally wounded and two slightly wounded, although one of the "mortally wounded" later recovered. The guerrillas left Livingston and three other men dead on the field. After loading about fifteen wounded into a government wagon, they retreated in a southwesterly direction and left the wounded at the small community of White Hare about ten miles from Stockton. News of Livingston's death was heralded in the Union press as far away as Kansas City.[79]

Most of the guerrillas rode south with Coffee to Cowskin Prairie in McDonald County, where they reorganized later in the month under his command, although some of Livingston's men, following a Captain Estes, were also reported to have joined Quantrill.[80]

According to legend, Livingston's body was buried in a cemetery at Stockton. Livingston's men learned of the location, and after the war some of them occasionally returned to visit the grave in secret. Another less credible story holds that the body was brought back to Sherwood and buried in the cemetery there. Long after the war was over, an old man was regularly seen laying flowers at the grave, which was marked by a big rock with just an "L" crudely etched on it.[81]

7
The War in Vernon County and the Burning of Nevada

In all of Missouri perhaps no area was more secessionist in sentiment before and during the Civil War than Vernon County. The results of the 1860 presidential election illustrate the depth of Southern sympathies prior to the war. Southern Democrat John C. Breckinridge received over half the 738 votes cast in Vernon County. Compromise candidates Stephen Douglas and John Bell split the remainder. Abraham Lincoln did not receive a single vote, although the author of the 1887 *History of Vernon County* admitted that "a dozen or so men in the county would have voted the Republican ticket had they been permitted."[1]

After the outbreak of hostilities the following spring, Southern sentiment in the county grew even more predominant. The 1887 history suggests that, after the Camp Jackson incident at St. Louis in May 1861, ninety-five percent of the citizens of the county sympathized with the Southern cause. "Vernon County," the author added, "was a miniature South Carolina in political sentiment."[2]

Situated on the border near Fort Scott, the county paid a high price for its disloyalty, as it became the theater for numerous skirmishes, raids, and counter raids throughout the war. The raid on Balltown in northern Vernon County in late August of 1861 by a body of Kansas troops from Fort Lincoln occasioned General Price's march toward Fort Scott and led indirectly to the action at Dry Wood. Then, after Price had gone north to Lexington, Doc Jennison's men raided into Vernon County, and Jim Lane burned the town of Osceola in neighboring St. Clair County.

These incursions caused great alarm in Vernon County, especially in the western half. Families thronged south in a mass exodus and took up temporary residence in northern Arkansas and extreme southern Missouri, abandoning their homeland to the Kansas troops and Confederate partisans, who sparred with each other in a deadly game of hide and seek. The frequent forays into Missouri by scouting parties from Fort Scott were often little more than a lark, and guerrillas holed up in the brush around their homes found equal sport in harassing vulnerable Union targets on both sides of the border.

Around the first of December 1861, William "Bill" Anderson in the company of Judge A.I. Baker and several other Southern sympathizers from around Anderson's home near Council Grove, Kansas, rode south to join Price's army, Baker having reportedly secured a major's commission from General Rains. They got as far as Vernon County, where they were camped on Dry Wood Creek, when they were attacked by a scouting party under Captain L.R. Jewell of the Sixth Kansas. One of the Rebels was killed, and Baker was captured. Anderson and the others escaped and proceeded to the Confederate recruiting camp near Osceola. After a few days there, Anderson struck for home, while Baker spent four months as a prisoner at Fort Lincoln. Upon his release he, too, went back to Council Grove and shortly afterwards killed Anderson's father in a dispute over a charge of horse stealing against the Andersons. Two months later, Anderson murdered Baker and fled for Missouri, where he joined Quantrill the next year and eventually earned the name "Bloody Bill."[3]

In February of 1862 Captain J.M. Gatewood returned from service in the Missouri State Guard to his home near Montevallo in southeast Vernon County and was assembling a company of guerrillas in the vicinity. When rumors of the recruiting activity reached Fort Scott, an eight-man scouting party under Lieutenant Reese Lewis of the Sixth Kansas was sent across the border to determine whether the reports were true and, if they were, to learn the exact location of the company.[4]

The scouting party ranged below Montevallo and then turned back toward Fort Scott. On the night of the 26th they camped at the home of a Union man named Riggs, who lived on the Little Dry Wood in western Vernon County. Seven soldiers stayed in the Riggs house while Lieutenant Lewis and another man retired to a nearby granary.

Confederate sympathizers in the area learned of the Federals' presence and by dawn had raised a bushwhacking party of seventeen men. Armed with double-barreled shotguns, the Rebels galloped onto the Riggs place just at daybreak and shot a Union corporal full of buckshot as he dashed out the front door with his musket to check on the commotion. They then blasted away at the house, firing through the window and open door, and nearly all the Federals inside received wounds of one sort or another.

Mr. Riggs and his kids sought refuge in the cellar, but the bedfast mother could not be moved. Miraculously she escaped injury, even as her bedposts splintered around her. Raising herself up amid the melee, she urged the soldiers not to surrender. The bushwhackers would run, she exclaimed, if the soldiers would just fight back.

Emboldened by the frail lady's exhortations, the soldiers dashed out of the house and returned fire, and Lieutenant Lewis and his companion charged up from the granary to join the fray. Just as Mrs. Riggs had predicted, the bushwhackers fled at the first sign of resistance and, according to the *History of Vernon County*, "were soon at their homes, engaged in their ordinary avocations, and more innocent looking men it would be difficult to find." Although all the Federals except the two who'd been in the granary received wounds of varying degrees, none died as a result of their injuries. None of the bushwhackers was seriously hurt.

The next day, February 28, Captain Harris S. Greeno from Fort Scott led a scouting party of fifty men into Vernon County looking for the bushwhackers responsible for the attack at the Riggs house. During their search, according to the county history, they "passed by the houses of and conversed with some of the very men who were in the attack the previous morning, without discovering their identity, of course." The Federals camped that night in Vernon County, and then rode back to Fort Scott the next day without having located the enemy.

Upon learning of the Riggs house fight and of the Federal search after the perpetrators, Captain Gatewood got his recruits together in the neighborhood of Montevallo, and when Captain Greeno returned on March 2, the Rebels trailed the Union scouting party much of the afternoon, looking for a chance to surprise and ambush the unsuspecting Federals. Finally, they managed to capture three soldiers from the scouting party who had stopped at a house, and they asked the men where their captain planned to camp that night. In an attempt to throw the Rebels off the trail, the Kansans said their comrades were going to camp at Montevallo.

Convinced by the lie, Gatewood immediately turned east in the direction of the village in hopes of discovering and attacking the Federal camp under cover of darkness. When he reached Montevallo, he discovered a number of horses hitched at his own house! Lights glimmered and voices of merriment wafted from the dwelling on the evening air. Supposing that the Yankees were camped there, he pulled out his revolver, dismounted his men, and advanced with them on foot toward the house.

He was about to order an attack on his own home when he discovered that the visitors were but a group of young people who had stopped by for a social gathering. Captain Gatewood walked back to his horse with his pistol in hand. As he was returning the weapon to its saddle holster, it accidentally discharged, and the ball passed downward through the captain's body. Gatewood collapsed and was carried into his house, where he soon died from his accidental, self-inflicted wound. Palled by the hapless turn of events, the Rebel company temporarily disbanded.

Brash young men from the area, however, continued to flock to the Confederate cause, and Union scouting parties were continually beating the bush for guerrillas. Two such scouting parties through Bates, Henry, St. Clair, and Vernon counties in April of 1862, for instance, resulted in one Rebel killed and another forty-nine taken prisoner. "Most of these men are of the worst, and ought to be hung," Brigadier General James Totten opined after learning of the capture of the guerrillas. "The whole wooded country of the Marais-des-Cygnes, Osage, and their tributaries is full of them."[5]

The area around Montevallo especially remained a hotbed of Southern sentiment. By mid-April a company of guerrillas under Henry Taylor, former sheriff of the county, had formed there; and a Union scout, composed of one hundred men of the First Iowa Cavalry and a detachment of the Eighth Missouri State Militia, was sent into the area from Osceola to try to break up the enemy company. On the evening of the 13th, the scouting party's commander, Lieutenant-Colonel Charles E. Moss, left his main force in camp five miles east of Montevallo while he and a group of twenty-eight men ventured into the village after dark and took up quarters at the Scobey Hotel.[6]

Although Taylor's Rebels had temporarily returned to their homes while awaiting orders, about twenty-five of them assembled during the night when word spread of the Federal occupation of the town. On the morning of the 14th at 4:30 a.m., the guerrillas surrounded the hotel and shouted for the Yankees to surrender or else they'd burn the house down around them. The Federal soldiers answered by opening fire, and a lively exchange of shot continued until near daylight, when the Southerners retreated to the rear of a store building about fifty yards away. When Colonel Moss ordered his men to rush out, form in a line, and charge, the Rebels overheard the command and dispersed without another shot.

Federal loss in the skirmish was two killed and six wounded.[7] The Rebels lost one man mortally wounded, "Irish Dan" Henley. Sometimes called the "Wild Irishman," Henley was known in St. Clair, Cedar, and Vernon counties, according to Colonel Moss, as "leader of the most desperate gangs of desperadoes in Missouri."[8] The guerrillas also had one man severely wounded and a couple of others slightly injured.

The next day Captain P. Gad Bryan rendezvoused with the main Federal force, and Colonel Moss sent one scouting party in the direction of Nevada and another under Captain Bryan in the opposite direction in search of the bushwhackers. The first party was unsuccessful, but Bryan came upon and skirmished with a part of the Rebels, killing one and seriously wounding another. The injured man turned out to be Wilson Maddox, keeper of the very hotel where the Federals had stayed the night before and one of the organizers of the Rebel ambush. Maddox, shot to pieces and left for dead, recovered, only to be killed a year later in Newton County.

When the scouts came in, they informed Colonel Moss that the Rebels were amassing for another possible assault on his command that evening at Montevallo. Moss responded by burning a good portion of the town, including the hotel where the previous attack had occurred, a tavern 300 yards away where the assault had been organized, and all the buildings in between. "This measure became necessary," Moss explained in his report of April 17, "as a precaution against attack and as a measure of safety, as those buildings, of little or no value to any one, were being used as places of protection and resort by the guerrillas."[9] Whether the incineration of the town had any deterrent effect on the Rebels is uncertain, but, for whatever reason, the anticipated second attack never occurred.

In August of 1862 the Enrolled Missouri Militia was created for the protection of the state and its citizens. Although controlled and paid by the state, the E.M.M. was armed and equipped by the Federal government, and it was expected to cooperate with Union military authorities in responding to emergency situations and in protecting citizens from brigands on either side of the war issue.

Bands of such outlaws abounded in Vernon County. The 1887 county history describes the situation that existed in early 1863:

> Back and forth into Missouri rode the Kansas jayhawkers; back and forth into Kansas rode the Missouri guerrillas; back and forth into loyal Cedar rode the Vernon bushwhackers; back and forth into rebel Vernon rode the Cedar militia. Every raid meant a robbery and plundering--maybe a house-burning and a murder.[10]

If any area of the state needed a peace-keeping force, it was Vernon County.

However, relations in the county were so tense and loyalties so divided that when a meeting was held at Nevada in March of 1863 to organize a local company of Enrolled Missouri Militia, a disagreement erupted among the fifty or so enlistees over the selection of a leader. Because all able-bodied males throughout the state were expected to enlist, many men who secretly sympathized with the South volunteered for the Enrolled Missouri Militia rather than expose their true sentiments. This appears to have been the case in Vernon County, where the men present at the organizational meeting chose as their captain Augustus Baker, whom the author of county history later called "a conservative Union man."[11]

Baker's chief rival in the election was John Frizzell, a staunch Unionist who lived near the Cedar County line and had served with the Cedar militia. Frizzell campaigned hard for the position of captain and took his defeat bitterly. According to the county history, he claimed he had been defeated by the "d----d rebels" and swore to get even.

In early May, he and a companion went to Baker's house and, upon a false show of complaisance, were readily admitted into the home. After stepping through the door, Frizzell suddenly drew his pistol and shot Baker down in the presence of his wife. The killers then sprang to their horses and rode away.[12]

As soon as word of the slaying reached Fort Scott, a detachment of Federal troops went out in search of the fugitives and located them at a home in Cedar County. Frizzell's accomplice escaped by leaping from an upstairs window, but the Kansas soldiers apprehended Frizzell and took him back to Fort Scott to stand trial for murder.

He claimed at his trial later in May that the accusation against him was a case of mistaken identity and that he had been in Cedar County at the time of the crime. A half dozen of his acquaintances, led by A.J. Pugh under whom Frizzell had served in the Cedar militia, trekked to Fort Scott to testify on his behalf, but to no avail. Based largely on the testimony of the victim's widow and another woman who happened to be at the Baker home at the time of the incident, Frizzell was found guilty and sentenced to hang on the 27th of the month.

When Frizzell's friends started back toward Cedar County on the 24th of the month, a Rebel scout brought word to guerrilla Captain William Marchbanks, camped on the Marmaton River, that a squad of Cedar County "milish" was headed down the road from Fort Scott to Nevada. Marchbanks and a desperate sidekick named Pony Hill set out after the "Feds" at the head of a small gang of bushwhackers and finally caught up with them at Nevada.

The guerrillas galloped onto the square yelling and shooting, and the militiamen scattered in every direction. All but two managed to escape. An unarmed old man named Shuey scurried on foot toward the shelter of a nearby house, but Pony Hill and another Rebel overtook him and shot him down in the dooryard over the supplications of the old man and pleas for mercy from several lady bystanders. Marchbanks caught up with the second victim, a man named Whitley, northwest of town and trapped him in a lane. After a brief exchange of fire, Marchbanks shot him out of the saddle. The guerrillas then retired to their camp on the Marmaton, while a few townspeople tended to the burial of Shuey and Whitley.

When Pugh and the rest of his party reached home and reported the attack, the militiamen of Cedar and St. Clair counties shrilled for revenge. The next day about a hundred well-armed and mounted men amassed and started for Vernon County under the command of Captain Anderson Morton. Intent on tracking down and either killing or capturing the Marchbanks gang, the militia camped the night of the 24th near Moore's Branch south of Nevada, where the guerrillas were thought to be hidden out.

Early the next morning, Morton and his men scoured the timber and brush along the creek but found no sign of the Rebels. The frustrated militiamen now turned their attention to the consolation prize of Nevada. The Federals knew that intelligence provided by spies in the town had led to Marchbanks's attack on Pugh and his men. Furthermore, citizens of the town had a long-standing reputation for furnishing the guerrillas with supplies and information. Nevada had danced to a disloyal tune since the beginning of the war, and, in the minds of the Federal militia, it was time for "the bushwhacker capital" to pay the piper.

It was not yet nine o'clock in the morning when the militia rode in from the south and took possession of Nevada. After a thorough search of the town turned up no bushwhackers, the Federals reassembled on the square. Captain Morton ordered that every house or building big enough to serve as a shelter for guerrillas be burned but that no plunder be taken and no peaceable citizen be hurt. The militia fanned out in small squads and carried out the order in methodical fashion. As commanded, they took no spoils, harmed no citizens, and insulted no women, but they were deaf to homeowners' protestations of innocence and pleas for special treatment. Tenants were given twenty minutes to remove their belongings, and then virtually every home and building in town was set ablaze.

The author of the 1887 *History of Vernon County* described the scene:

> Soon bright flames flashed from the burning buildings all over the town. Volumes of black, thick smoke rolled up into the blue May-day sky, until swept away by the May breezes. Pillars of cloud and fire shot towards the zenith until bent and broken by the currents of the upper air. The door yards and vacant lots were piled with household articles, around which wailed and mourned, or scolded and stormed, the dispossessed women as they kept the flying brands from their goods, or quarreled with the torch-bearers. Soon the roofs fell in, the skeletons of the stout hardwood frames stood out like livid bars of iron, and a fierce heat went up like the glow of a Babylonian furnace.[13]

In all, about seventy-five homes were fired. The courthouse, too, and all the businesses in town were put to the torch. Only about a dozen dwellings were spared, notably those belonging to citizens who had won favor with the Federals by taking care of the dead bodies of Shuey and Whitley. By 11:00 a.m. the town was already a smoldering ruins. With the signature of their fiery work spiraling in black clouds of smoke across the sky behind them, Captain Morton and his men formed in a line and marched out of Nevada on the Montevallo road.

Ignorant of Captain Morton's presence at Nevada, a group of about twenty-five bushwhackers gathered in southeast Vernon County on May 25, the very morning of the fire, for a foray into Cedar County, where they raided Union settlements, stealing horses, firing houses, and taking plunder. According to the 1887 *History of Vernon County*, "Among the houses burned was that of old man Shuey, then lying a corpse in Nevada City."[13]

The county history goes on to say, "While Nevada City was burning the bushwhackers were returning to Vernon with the trophies of their raid." The guerrillas disbanded at the home of William Gabbert southwest of Montevallo, but about a dozen of them lingered to rest and take dinner after their tiring ride.

As Captain Morton and his militia rode away from the smoldering ruins of Nevada and marched down the Montevallo road, they spotted a fresh trail where the bushwhackers had crossed the road upon their return from Cedar County. Morton immediately set out on the trail and caught the guerrillas at Gabbert's house by complete surprise. "Morton and his men," says the county history, "shot some of them dead so quickly that they scarcely knew what hurt them. Others ran wildly and aimlessly about and were shot down as they ran. A few escaped by running to the brush and dodging a swarm of bullets sent after them." In all, the militia left seven bushwhackers dead on the ground and a couple of others slightly wounded. The Federals had just one man injured, and they recovered most of the plunder that had been taken by the guerrillas in Cedar County that morning.[15]

About July 1, 1863, Lieutenant Colonel Charles W. Blair, post commander at Fort Scott, dispatched four companies of the Third Wisconsin Cavalry to preserve the peace in western Vernon County and to set up outposts from which to operate against bushwhackers in the eastern part of the county and in other areas of western Missouri. A detachment of the Third Wisconsin marched north from Dry Wood Creek on the 7th of the month and came upon a guerrilla camp the next day in northern Vernon County near the confluence of the Marmaton and Osage rivers, breaking up the camp and scattering the bushwhackers in every direction. According to Major E.A. Calkins, commander of the Third Wisconsin, five of the Rebels were killed and three severely wounded, one of whom was "the noted guerrilla Pony Hill." Henry Taylor was also reported injured in the affray.[16]

Later in the summer, after Quantrill's notorious raid on Lawrence, Kansas, General Thomas Ewing, Jr., commanding the District of the Border, issued Order Number 11, aimed at destroying the guerrillas' network of civilian support in western Missouri. The order decreed that all citizens living in the northern half of Vernon County and all of Bates, Cass, and Jackson counties remove to within one mile of a Federal installation or else leave the district and that all forage and grain remaining in the district after fifteen days would be destroyed. Effects of the order were felt most severely in Cass and Bates counties, which were depopulated almost overnight, and the region became known as the "Burnt District."

The order did not have as much effect in Vernon County, because most of the people in the proscribed area had already left. The provision of the decree relating to the destruction of grain also had little consequence in the county, because, according to the 1887 history, "By that time there was none left to burn."[17]

Despite its lack of a noticeably dramatic effect in Vernon County, Order Number 11 combined with the presence of the Third Wisconsin to reduce Rebel activity in the area to a series of sporadic, minor incidents. Throughout the remainder of the war, bushwhackers streaked across the Vernon County stage in a desperate parody of earlier dramas, but their Rebel yells and the sounds of their guns were just a faint echo of the fierce guerrilla fighting of 1862 and 1863.

7
Quantrill and the
Massacre at Baxter Springs

Of all the Confederate guerrilla forces in Missouri during the Civil War, the most notorious was that of William C. Quantrill. Born in Ohio, Quantrill moved to Kansas Territory in 1857, and during the scholastic term of 1858-1859, he taught school at Stanton in Miami County. Shortly afterward, Quantrill adopted the alias Charley Hart and fell in briefly with rabid abolitionists around Lawrence, although it's doubtful he ever sincerely shared their antislavery zeal. More likely, he merely used the unrest of the times as an excuse for banditry. At any rate, he soon ran afoul of the law. Facing arrest by Kansas authorities, he underwent a dubious change of heart.[1]

On a mission into Missouri to liberate slaves, he betrayed his cohorts to the slave owner and took up the cause of the South. When war broke out, he followed Price's army to southern Missouri, where he presumably participated in the Battles of Carthage and Wilson's Creek.

Acting more from selfish motives, say critics, than from political conviction, Quantrill formed a small band of guerrillas upon his return to the Jackson County area in the late fall of 1861 and began to harass Union targets around Independence. Brash Southern boys in and around Jackson County flocked to the rising guerrilla leader, and by the following summer Quantrill was already the most noted bushwhacker in the state and the chief adversary of Federal officials in the Kansas City area.

After a summer of raiding in Jackson County and across the border into Kansas, Quantrill's guerrilla band of 150 men started south in early November of 1862. On the evening of the 5th, in northern Barton County the guerrillas fell in with 300 Confederates under Colonel Warner Lewis, who proposed an attack on the Eighth

Missouri Militia detachment at Lamar. When Quantrill learned the Federals were garrisoned in the courthouse, he balked at the idea of assailing a brick building.

Nevertheless, he circled the town as planned and came in from the south about 8:00 p.m., driving in the Union pickets. Colonel Lewis, who was supposed to strike from the north, failed to show, but the bushwhackers launched an assault on their own. For over two hours they fired away at the courthouse and other houses and buildings where the militia had taken shelter, killing three Federals and seriously wounding three others. The guerrillas themselves lost at least two and perhaps as many as six men. Finally, Quantrill, frustrated that he could inflict no greater casualties, burned about a third of the town, then resumed the march south.[2]

During the winter, Quantrill made a trip to the Confederate capital at Richmond, Virginia, in futile quest of a colonel's commission under the Partisan Rangers Act. Back in Missouri the following spring, Quantrill reunited with the men whom he'd attached to General John S. Marmaduke's regular Confederate troops, and together the small guerrilla command started north toward its old stomping grounds of Jackson County. Passing near Stockton in Cedar County on Sunday, April 19, 1863, the band of about thirty guerrillas came upon seven local soldiers of the Eighth Missouri State Militia Cavalry, who were on their way home after accompanying a paymaster to Springfield. The bushwhackers captured the Union men and lined them up on the road. After stripping the men of their clothes except for their undershirts and drawers, the guerrillas opened fire. All seven soldiers dropped to the ground in a heap and died instantly. The victims were Michael Horbeck, Peter Pike, Nathan Reason, James Williams, a man named Dalton, and two unidentified men.[3]

Continuing their journey, the Quantrill band came upon Rob Williams and a man named Powell north of Stockton. The guerrillas took the two men prisoner and forced them to escort the gang to the nearby home of a Southern sympathizer. Quantrill hoped to secure food for his men and horses, but when the motley troupe reached the house, they found no forage. The bushwhackers demanded that Williams tell them where they might get feed, but while he was standing and delivering the desired information, one of them shot him in the head, killing him instantly.[4]

The guerrillas then turned to Powell and opened fire, wounding him, but he, nevertheless, sprang up and dashed three-quarters of a mile before the gang overtook him. He dropped to his knees and pled for his life, but the merciless bushwhackers finished him off with a second shot. After taking a gun off the body, the killers went to the dead man's home, where they were met by several women. "You have ruined us," one of the ladies cried.

"We have killed them and you cannot help yourselves," a coldhearted member of the gang replied.

In the northwest part of the county, the guerrillas came to the home of Obadiah Smith, a Baptist minister and state representative from Cedar County, who had recently returned from a legislative session in Jefferson City. Long after the war, former guerrilla John McCorkle claimed that Smith was also a "heartless old murderer…who had done much murdering and burning in that part of the state." Although this appears to be an exaggeration at best, Smith did serve at one time as a guide for the Kansas Brigade, and he also helped organize a home guard force in the Cedar County area to combat bushwhackers.[6]

The fifty-six-year-old Smith was out in his garden when the guerrillas rode up, and Quantrill summoned him to the fence. Thinking the bushwhackers were Union soldiers because of the Federal uniforms they wore, Smith obliged. He carried with him a Sharp's rifle and a pistol.

Quantrill shook hands with Smith and said his men were Kansas troops. Then he gave the rifle an admiring glance. "You have a gun just like mine," the guerrilla leader remarked.

Smith said proudly that the rifle had been given to him by Senator Jim Lane, commanding general of the Kansas Brigade.

This surely infuriated Quantrill, as Lane was also a noted jayhawker. Archenemy of the bushwhackers, he'd carried out the raid on Osceola in 1861. "Let me see it," the guerrilla chief suggested as he continued to eye the weapon.

As Smith unsuspectingly handed over the gun, he boasted, according to McCorkle, of the number of Rebels he'd killed with it. Quantrill took the gun and immediately leveled it at its owner. "I'll give you the contents of this gun!" the chieftain exclaimed as he pulled the trigger. The shot either missed its mark or the weapon misfired. Smith managed to draw his revolver and open fire on the guerrillas, knocking two of them out of the saddle.[7]

He then dashed toward his house, and his wife, forty-one-year-old Eliza, hurried to intervene. She got between her husband and the guerrillas and momentarily deterred their pursuit. By the time the bushwhackers got past her, Smith had rounded the corner of the house and struck out across an orchard trying to escape. He had almost reached a fence on the other side of the lot when a guerrilla named Bill McGuire overtook him and shot him dead with a single bullet. McGuire's enraged comrades rode up and emptied their revolvers into Smith's lifeless body. After shooting him repeatedly in the back, they turned him over and shot him several more times in the face.[8]

The gang then took seven or eight hundred dollars off the corpse and threw the empty wallet toward the grieving widow as they galloped away. On their way out of the county, they shot one last victim, a man named McWaters, and then crossed into Henry County. The Cedar County militia mounted a pursuit but failed to overtake the bushwhackers.[9]

Upon reaching Jackson County, Quantrill holed up in the Sni Hills for most of the summer, but on August 21, 1863, he led his band on the most notorious guerrilla raid of the war, the Lawrence Massacre, which some of the bushwhackers justified by citing Lane's destruction of Osceola. In all, the bloodthirsty Rebels, many of them enraged over the deaths of five Southern girls eight days earlier in the collapse of a Union prison, gunned down at least 160 civilians and approximately twenty unarmed Union recruits during the slaughter.

Although chased by Federal troops all the way to Missouri, most of the guerrillas made it back unharmed and scattered into the Sni Hills of eastern Jackson County. Six weeks later Quantrill called a rendezvous for the march south to winter quarters, and about 350 guerrillas responded. The command was organized as the First Regiment, First Brigade, Army of the South, although there's no evidence that Quantrill was ever officially commissioned as a colonel in the Confederate Army.

At the rendezvous, too, were Colonel John D. Holt and about 100 raw recruits who'd accompanied Quantrill to Lawrence and were now on their way south to join the Confederate Army. Although just a temporary adjunct to the guerrilla command, Holt's company brought the total number of men gathered for the march south to 450, about the same number who'd ridden to Lawrence, which was the largest number of men ever assembled during the war under a single guerrilla leader.

On the morning of October 2, 1863, the journey south began from the Perdee farm on the Blackwater River in Johnson County, the same point from which the march to Lawrence had commenced. Near the Fort Scott-Nevada area the guerrillas captured and killed two furloughed soldiers of the Fourteenth Kansas Cavalry, but the four-day march through western Missouri was otherwise uneventful. On the night of October 5, Quantrill camped on Shoal Creek near Grand Falls just southwest of present-day Joplin. The next morning the guerrillas struck west toward Baxter Springs, Kansas, aiming to pick up the military road for the march to winter quarters in Texas.[10]

As early as 1862 the Union army had established temporary camps at Baxter Springs as a stopover point for supply trains from Fort Scott to Fort Gibson in Indian Territory or to Fort Smith in Arkansas. In addition to providing security for the trains, the camps at Baxter Springs served as outposts for troops to operate against Rebels in the area.

In July of 1863, shortly after the departure from the area of Colonel James Williams's First Kansas Colored Infantry, Union officials decided to establish a permanent garrison at Baxter Springs. In August, work began on a fort one-half mile west of Spring River near the current site of the town's historical museum. By early October the fort consisted just of some log cabins facing east toward the river. The cabins served as both barracks and blockhouse and had a total frontage of about 100 feet. The area behind or immediately west of the cabins was enclosed by a four-foot high breastwork of earth and logs that provided additional fortification.

Up until the 4th of October the garrison consisted of one company of the Second Kansas Colored Regiment commanded by Lieutenant R.E. Cook and part of Company D, Third Wisconsin Cavalry. On the 4th, Lieutenant James B. Pond arrived with part of Company C, Third Wisconsin, to take command of the post, which he named Fort Blair in honor of Lieutenant-Colonel Charles W. Blair of the Fourteenth Kansas (although it was known familiarly as Fort Baxter).[11]

The next day Pond ordered the west wall of the breastwork knocked out so that the enclosed fortification behind the cabins could be expanded to accommodate the increased number of soldiers now assigned to the garrison. In anticipation of the expansion, Pond located his tent beyond the open, west end of the breastwork. A kitchen area was situated about 200 feet south of the fortification near Spring Branch, a small tributary of Spring River.

On the morning of October 6, Pond sent out about sixty of his best men, along with all the horses and wagons, on a foraging party. Left at the camp were about twenty-five men from Pond's Company C, twenty from Company D, and fifty troops from the black regiment. About 11:30 Lieutenant Cook and seven other men including Johnny Fry, a former pony express rider, went to the Spring River timber to take target practice

Quantrill approached the fort about noon. Near the crossing of Spring River, his advance guard under Dave Pool and John Brinker spotted tracks of a wagon train and sent scouts ahead to try to determine the location and nature of the train. The scouts found a Federal camp not far beyond the river but did not realize there was a fort nearby, apparently having discovered just the cooking camp or an auxiliary detail, perhaps Lieutenant Cook and his men or one of the foraging parties.

When the scouts dropped back to report their findings, Quantrill brought up the main column and divided the command for an assault on the encampment. He ordered Pool and Brinker to take half the men (about 150, according to Quantrill's report of October 13) and attack the camp from the east. Meanwhile, Quantrill himself took the other half and moved off through the woods to the north with the apparent intention of attacking from that direction.[12]

Pool and Brinker hoisted a Federal flag as a decoy and, supported by a company under William Gregg, approached the camp in three columns from the east and south. The Rebels came upon a Federal wagon and shot the teamster. About the same time, they discovered Lieutenant Cook's detachment, demanded the group's surrender, and promptly shot Cook, Johnny Fry, and one other man when they did not immediately comply. The other five soldiers were put under guard, but, because of the risk of further alarming the Federal camp, they were not shot. (Two of these men later escaped, and the other three were released.)[13]

When the guerrillas learned of the nearby Federal garrison from one of the prisoners, they promptly bolted out of the woods toward the fort. Most of the Federals were at the cooking camp relaxing and enjoying their noon meal when the Rebels came charging across the clearing. Although at least a few soldiers had heard the firing at the river, the disturbance did not cause a general alarm, because the noise was mistaken as the recreational shooting of Cook's men.

Several Federals, whose fortuitous sinking spells had helped them dodge foraging duty earlier in the day, were now lying in the blockhouse on sick call. At the sounds of attack, the puny warriors at the bulwark quickly revived and tried to mount a defense.

However, the Federals at the cooking camp were taken by surprise, and the guerrillas overran the garrison before the lolling soldiers had time to react. Firing their weapons and screaming like demons, many of the Rebels galloped between the blockhouse and the kitchen area to cut off the soldiers from the fortified entrenchment, where they'd left their arms 200 feet away. The startled Federals made a mad dash through enemy lines, racing in front of and behind Rebel horses in a desperate effort to reach the fort. Four were gunned down in the attempt, but the rest managed to reach their weapons and the relative protection of the breastwork.

Some of the bushwhackers, though, rode right into the entrenchment, and the close quarters fighting was hot and heavy with bullets zinging through the air and thunking into the earthen embankment. Lieutenant Pond himself had to dash through the guerrilla ranks to get inside the rampart, where, in his own words, "I found the enemy's men as numerous as my own."[14]

Pond managed to rally his troops, and the Federals soon drove the guerrillas outside the crude fort. The two sides kept up a furious exchange until the Rebels finally dropped back to reorganize. They faced the fortification in a line of battle and kept up a sporadic gunfire even as they plotted another attack.

Pond yelled for his men to retrieve the twelve-pound mountain howitzer that he had brought from Fort Scott two days earlier and that now set just outside the breastwork on the north side. Not a single man answered the call. Either the men didn't hear the command above the din of battle or, like Shakespeare's Falstaff, they decided that discretion was the better part of valor and chose to ignore the order. Pond, in his report a few days later, was inclined to give his men the benefit of the doubt "as the volleys of musketry and the yells of the enemy nearly drowned every other noise."[15]

When none of his men heeded his call, the dogged Pond leaped over the parapet himself and got in position to operate the howitzer. Although he'd never worked the big gun before, he got it loaded and trained it on the largest cluster of guerrillas surrounding the fort.

Meanwhile, Quantrill, with his half of the guerrilla command, spotted a Union force out on the prairie beyond a hill north of the fort. As Quantrill began forming his men in a line facing the Federals at the edge of the timber along Spring River, he heard heavy firing off to his left and rode out to investigate, shielded from the Federals' view by the ridge. He saw the fort for the first time and discovered half of his command busily engaged there, but a more compelling enemy loomed over the crest of the hill. Quantrill called off his men at the fort to reinforce those poised for battle at the edge of the woods, where his lieutenants were still trying to determine the size and character of the enemy that faced them.

The Federal force, over 100 strong, was the wagon train of Major General James G. Blunt, commander of the District of the Frontier headquartered at Fort Scott. Earlier in the year Blunt's old Department of Kansas headquartered at Fort Leavenworth had been dissolved, and in the re-organization Blunt had been assigned to the District of the Frontier. It was a far-flung field of authority encompassing the southern part of Kansas below the 38th parallel, the western tier of Missouri counties below the same line, all of Indian Territory, and the western tier of Arkansas counties, but it was considered a less prestigious post.

On October 4th Blunt had received word at Fort Scott that Fort Smith was being threatened by a superior Confederate force, and he set out that day to reinforce the latter place, taking with him eight wagons loaded with supplies and all the records and papers belonging to the headquarters, as he planned to make Fort Smith his temporary command center.

He also brought along several members of his staff, including Major H.Z. Curtis, assistant adjutant-general and son of Major-General Samuel Curtis; Major Benjamin S. Henning, provost marshal of the district; Lieutenant John E. Tappan, aide-de-camp; and Lieutenant Asa W. Farr, judge-advocate. Also accompanying the general were the wagon drivers, several clerks and orderlies from his headquarters, a fourteen-member brigade band outfitted in new uniforms and riding in a new bandwagon, a twelve-year-old drummer boy and servant of the band leader, an artist-correspondent for Frank Leslie's weekly newspaper, and a young lady named Lydia

Thomas who was on her way from Topeka to Fort Gibson to join her ill husband, the brigade quartermaster.

The escort consisted of forty men of Company I of the Third Wisconsin Cavalry under Lieutenant H.D. Banister and forty-five men of Company A of the Fourteenth Kansas Cavalry under Lieutenant Robert H. Pierce. Lieutenant Josiah G. Cavert of the Third Wisconsin had overall command of the escort.

On the morning of October 6, the Federals marched the final twenty miles of their journey and approached Baxter Springs about noon. On the prairie north of Fort Blair near the present-day site of Baxter Springs High School, the march halted at Willow Creek to let the scattered rear close ranks so that the train could present a suitable military appearance on its approach to the camp.

The pause had continued for almost fifteen minutes and the order to resume the march had just been given when the Federals spotted about 100 horsemen emerging from the woods over a quarter mile to the east. The riders advanced at a walk until they were within about 300 yards, where they drew up in line. Because almost all of them were dressed in Federal blue, General Blunt at first assumed them to be some of Lieutenant Pond's cavalry on drill, returning from a scout, or sent out to greet him. His suspicion, however, was aroused when he noticed confusion among the ranks and saw several men, whom he presumed to be officers, riding up and down the line in an apparent effort to organize the troops.

Blunt sent out William Tough, his chief scout and a noted Kansas Red Leg, who reported back that the riders were an enemy force and that an engagement was taking place at the fort not more than 400 yards away. The Federals, though, could not see the camp nor hear the sounds of battle because of the intervening swell of ground. Alighting from his buggy to mount his horse, Blunt ordered the escort into a line of battle and then rode out himself about fifty yards until he could hear the firing at the fort.

At about the same time, Major Henning spotted riders coming over the crest of the hill from the direction of the camp angling northeast across the prairie to reinforce those facing the Federal escort. Henning, the scout Tough, and a soldier named Wheeler rode forward to the brow of the hill and saw the fighting at the camp, which was virtually surrounded by the enemy. Stragglers, though, continued to withdraw from the engagement to reinforce Quantrill out on the prairie. Major Henning's party immediately opened fire on a group of the laggards and received their fire in return.

As the group passed on, Henning noticed another group of five guerrillas herding three Federal prisoners away from the fort and heading along the same path the other stragglers had followed. While Tough rode back to report to General Blunt, Henning and Wheeler charged the party with guns blazing, dispersing the guerrillas and liberating their comrades. In so doing, they killed one of Quantrill's men and wounded another. The Rebels in turn fired on the prisoners and wounded one as the captives made their escape. Henning's skirmish with the guerrillas had taken him over the crest of the hill. When he turned to go back to the Federal line, he discovered it was too late.

Most of the guerrillas at the fort had welcomed the opportunity to fight an exposed enemy out on the open prairie rather than renew a dubious assault on an entrenched position, and Quantrill now had about 150 men formed at the Spring River timber to reinforce the line of riders who had already advanced onto the prairie. With the odds sufficiently in his favor, the Rebel chieftain ordered an attack.

The guerrillas rode forward at a walk, keeping up a sporadic fire. When they were within about 200 yards, two soldiers of Company A in the Federal line turned to run. Major Curtis and other officers drove them back into line, but no sooner had the officers returned to their positions than the same two men and about eight others turned and fled. Seeing the panic in the Union line, Quantrill ordered an all-out charge.

When General Blunt, from his forward position, turned in the saddle to give his escort the order to fire, he was startled to see his line already broken. According to his report of October 19, his troops were "in full gallop over the prairie, completely panic-stricken." It was, according to Blunt, a "disorderly and disgraceful retreat."[16]

Seeing the attack and realizing he was cut off from his own line, Major Henning made a desperate dash for the Federal fort. Hotly pursued by screaming guerrillas, he galloped toward the fortification, waving his hat frantically to signal that he was a friend, and he managed to get inside the bulwark.

He found Lieutenant Pond still manning the howitzer just outside the breastwork. The first shot fell well short of the mark, but just the threat of the big gun quickly dispersed the cluster of guerrillas who remained at the fort. Two more rounds soon persuaded them to retire from the fray, and they straggled off to join their comrades on the prairie rather than engage an artillery piece with six-shooters.

Out on the prairie, as the shrieking guerrillas came stampeding toward the Federals, Company A was already in full retreat, many of them having discarded their weapons without even firing them. The men of Company I, though, stood their ground and fired a full volley when the Rebels were within about sixty yards. The barrage momentarily checked the right side of the Rebel line, but the shots were "too high to hurt any one," according to Quantrill's report. The bullets hissed harmlessly in the air above the heads of the charging guerrillas. The left side of their line never broke stride, and the right quickly rallied.[17]

Company I, too, now turned to run, and, according to Quantrill, the Federals "fled in the wildest confusion on the prairie." The battle was now just a horse race that the more poorly mounted Federals were destined to lose. In the words of the laconic Quantrill, "We closed up on them, making fearful havoc on every side."[18]

No wonder Quantrill didn't go into particulars! The so-called battle quickly turned into a massacre. The superbly mounted guerrillas overtook the fleeing Federals out on the prairie and shot them down like frontiersmen slaughtering a herd of buffalo. Many of the soldiers who thought to escape by outdistancing their pursuers were betrayed by a deep ravine that paralleled the road west of where the attack occurred. The fast-charging Rebels closed on the frantic Federals and gunned them down at the ditch as they attempted to cross. Other soldiers threw up their arms in supplication, only to be executed with a bullet through the head after their surrender. Many of those killed in such a manner were shot a second and a third time for good measure. The guerrillas would not be burdened with prisoners.[19]

Lieutenant Farr was one of the first men killed. He was riding in a carriage when the attack began. Unarmed, he sprang from the vehicle and dashed on foot across the prairie, trying to escape. He didn't get far before tumbling to the ground beneath a hail of bullets and a load of buckshot.

General Blunt, better mounted than most of his men, made a mad gallop across the prairie toward the ravine. As his powerful horse vaulted the ditch, the general was tossed from the saddle, but he clung to the animal's neck and mane until it had carried him to safety. During his "run for life," according to General Blunt, "revolver bullets flew around my head thick as hail."[20]

General James G. Blunt, whose wagon train was annihilated at Baxter Springs. *Courtesy J. Dale West.*

Mrs. Thomas was riding in a buggy at the time of the attack. When the firing started, she turned to the driver of the buggy, an orderly named Charles Davis. "What are we going to do?" she cried.[21]

"Get away from here if we can," Davis shouted.

He got the team turned around and started racing back toward Fort Scott. He told Mrs. Thomas to get on the floorboard beneath the seat, and he, too, got on his knees and leaned as low as he could as he applied the whip. Bullets riddled the top of the buggy, but neither driver nor passenger was hit. The exhausted horses finally came to a halt after a run of about three miles.

Davis spotted two horses with empty saddles racing toward him and managed to halt them. He led one up to the side of the buggy, and Mrs. Thomas leaped onto its saddle. Davis then mounted the other one, and they galloped away again. After riding another half mile or so, they spotted a cluster of mounted men about three-quarters of a mile away. Approaching cautiously, they discovered the group was General Blunt and a small party of Federals who had managed to escape. Blunt detailed a soldier to accompany Mrs. Thomas to Fort Scott, and she arrived there safely late the next day.

Had the guerrillas known of Mrs. Thomas's presence from the beginning, she very likely would have been safe in any case.[22] The elevation of womanhood was at the very center of the guerrilla creed.[23] In Barton's *Three Years with Quantrill*, former guerrilla John McCorkle, in speaking of the Baxter Springs battle, declared that, when he and his comrades spotted a woman riding in a carriage, they held their fire. The lady to whom he referred was presumably Mrs. Thomas. Even at Lawrence, where over 160 men were slaughtered, Quantrill gave strict orders that no woman should be molested.

When the attack began, Major Curtis, like General Blunt, raced toward the ravine. He was out in front of his pursuers and about to make his getaway when his horse was shot as it gathered itself to leap over the gully. The major was thrown to the ground as the animal pitched forward into the ditch and then scrambled away. When one of the Rebels rode up and ordered the major to surrender, he ignored the pleas of a nearby Union soldier that he not let himself be taken prisoner. Instead, he handed over his weapon. The bushwhacker promptly shot Curtis with his own gun. Mistaking the major's identity, apparently because of the fancy officer's uniform he wore, the guerrilla shouted, "I've killed Blunt; I've killed the old son of a bitch."[24]

A few soldiers who were shot lived to tell the story. Sergeant Jack Splane surrendered upon a promise that he would be treated as a prisoner of war. When he handed over his arms, his captor said,

"Tell old God that the last man you saw on earth was Quantrill." Then the Rebel leveled his revolver and filled Splane with bullets, but the sergeant miraculously survived.[25]

Private Jesse Smith had a similar tale to tell. Despite being shot several times, he never lost consciousness, and he related his experience to Major Henning, who recorded it the next day in his report. According to Smith, while he lay face down on the prairie, the guerrilla who shot him "jumped upon his back and essayed to dance, uttering the most vile imprecations."[26]

When Frank Arnold had his horse shot from under him at the beginning of the attack, guerrillas swept down upon him demanding his surrender. Arnold handed over his revolver and was promptly shot four times: in the left arm, in the face, in the right arm, and in one of his fingers. Feigning death, he lay for some time before another group of bushwhackers approached and discovered his deception. One of them lowered his revolver and pulled the trigger, but the hammer snapped on an empty chamber. Hearing the sound, Arnold opened one eye and saw the guerrilla placing fresh caps. As the guerrilla lowered the barrel of his pistol again, Arnold closed his eyes and prepared for death. The gun exploded, a second ball slammed into Arnold's face, and his mind went dark. Regaining consciousness later in the evening, he was carried into camp, where he rallied the following day, despite his severe wounds and loss of blood.[27]

When the assault began, the driver of the band wagon struck west-southwest across the prairie pursued by a small party of guerrillas that included William Bledsoe. (Most of the Rebels were chasing the escort, who fled mainly to the northwest.) When Bledsoe shouted for the fugitives to surrender, one of them poked a revolver out of the wagon and shot him. The wagon raced on for about half a mile when it hit a bump and a wheel flew off, bringing the carriage to a careening halt. The frantic band members waved white handkerchiefs in gestures of surrender, but the Rebels rode up and shot them without preamble. Years later, guerrillas such as McCorkle and Gregg suggested that the band members would have been spared if Bledsoe had not been killed, but the day's other events belie such an assertion.

Slain along with the band members were the drummer boy and the newspaper correspondent. After they and the band members had been shot, all the bodies were tossed in and under the wagon, and the carriage was set ablaze. The fire brought the twelve-year-old lad back to consciousness, and he tried to crawl away, his clothes burning and melting away from his body as he dragged himself through the tall grass. He collapsed and died thirty feet away. The wagon and the bodies of the soldiers were partly consumed by the fire before it burned itself out.

The few soldiers of the escort who managed to escape were pursued up to three or four miles before the guerrillas called off the chase. The Rebels rode back to the scene of the attack and spent the better part of the afternoon celebrating their dreadful victory. After thoroughly ransacking the Federal wagons and supplies, they set afire everything they could not carry off or use for their own purposes. They confiscated a demijohn of whiskey from General Blunt's carriage, and Quantrill himself got roaring drunk and rode about the battlefield boasting of his bloody conquest. "By God," he gloated, "Shelby could not whip Blunt; neither could Marmaduke, but I whipped him." Gregg claimed it was the first time he ever saw Quantrill drunk.[28]

After sampling more than his share of the whiskey, a hot-blooded young guerrilla named Riley Crawford walked up to the body of one of the soldiers and prodded the man with a sword he had captured. "Get up, you Federal son of a bitch!" Crawford shouted.[29]

To everyone's utter surprise, the man jumped up as commanded and faced his accuser. The soldier was not even wounded and had simply feigned death to escape detection, but now, assuming his ruse had been discovered, he leaped to his feet. Crawford promptly brought out his revolver and shot the man.

General Blunt managed to rally about fifteen of his runaway soldiers. Six, including Lieutenant Tappan, he sent to Fort Scott to report the massacre and to procure reinforcements. With the remaining nine soldiers, he lurked in the nearby woods, watching as the guerrillas burned the wagons. At one point the bushwhackers spotted him and feigned an attack but dropped back when they were unable to surround Blunt's small party.

Around two o'clock George Todd, Quantrill's second-in-command, approached the fort bearing a flag of truce. He said that he was acting in the name of Colonel Quantrill, First Regiment, First Brigade, Army of the South, and he demanded the surrender of the camp. When Lieutenant Pond refused, Todd proposed an exchange of prisoners. Pond said he had no prisoners but that he had seen several wounded guerrillas fall from their horses and he would take care of them if Todd would do the same for the Federal prisoners. Todd agreed, saying that Major Curtis and twelve other soldiers were being held captive and that no harm would come to them if the lieutenant would care for the wounded guerrillas and parole them when they were able to leave. Todd's statement, of course, was a mere subterfuge to try to gain additional information, as Major Curtis and the others had already been executed.

Late in the afternoon, the guerrillas formed on the prairie south of the fort to resume their march. Todd and "Bloody Bill" Anderson urged another assault on the fort, but Quantrill refused, because, in his own words, "I did not think it prudent...as we had wounded men already to carry, and it was so far to bring them." The Rebels loaded William Bledsoe's body and the wounded John Koger into a Federal wagon and about 5 p.m., according to Quantrill, "took up the line of march due south on the old Texas road."[30]

After sending Lieutenant Tappan to Fort Scott, General Blunt had dispatched messengers to inform Federal authorities at Fort Gibson and other points south of the massacre and alert them of Quantrill's presence in the area. When the Rebels resumed their march, he also sent scouts to follow the retreat, and they trailed the guerrillas as far south as the Neosho River before returning to the fort.

Lieutenant Tappan arrived at Fort Scott about four o'clock on the morning of October 7, and within an hour Lieutenant Colonel Charles W. Blair set out with five companies of infantry and 100 cavalry to reinforce General Blunt. Bodies were still being carried in for burial and graves were being dug when the colonel arrived at Baxter Springs on the afternoon of October 8. "It was a fearful sight," he lamented in his report of October 15. "Some 85 bodies, nearly all shot through the head, most of them shot from five to seven times each, horribly mangled, charred and blackened by fire."[31]

Major Henning's official report shows eighty Federal soldiers killed and eighteen wounded, including six killed and ten wounded during the attack on the fort. These figures essentially agree with the calculations of Lieutenant Pond and General Blunt, although the post surgeon reported a total of 101 killed, including eight at the fort. Union estimates of enemy casualties, on the other hand, seem greatly exaggerated. Henning, for instance, placed the number of guerrillas killed and wounded at between twenty and thirty.

Quantrill's own statement of his loss is probably closer to the truth. In his report to General Price, Quantrill said he had one man killed (Bledsoe) and one wounded (Koger) during the attack on Blunt's escort and two killed (Robert Ward and William Lotspeach) and two wounded (Lieutenant Toothman and Private Thomas Hill) during the fight at the fort. W.H. Warner, the post surgeon, confirmed that the number of guerrillas killed at the fort was two.

Quantrill further asserted with reasonable accuracy that out of Blunt's total escort of approximately 125 men, the guerrillas left only about forty of them alive. Quantrill, however, did overestimate the number of Federals killed at the fort, claiming sixteen killed when the actual number was about half that figure. He was also mistaken in certain other details, believing, for instance, that General Blunt and Major Henning were among the dead.

Although junior officers such as Lieutenant Pond praised Blunt for his gallantry in hanging on the enemy's flank with a mere handful of men, public opinion was less generous. In the October 17, 1863 issue of the *Kansas City Daily Journal of Commerce*, for instance, editor T. Dwight Thacher cited a report from a *Leavenworth Times* correspondent claiming that General Blunt was remiss for carrying almost all of his ammunition in the wagons in boxes with the lids screwed on rather than allowing the soldiers to carry it in their cartridge boxes. Thacher further censured the general for not having sent scouts out while traveling through a territory known to be infested with guerrillas. Blunt's carelessness, said the editor, "is undoubtedly one of the wickedest military neglects that has happened in our country since the war."

General Blunt's military career suffered considerably from such criticism, but he largely restored his reputation during Price's invasion of Missouri in the fall of 1864. After the war Blunt returned to private life and died years later in a Washington, D.C. mental hospital.

The bodies of the dead soldiers at Baxter Springs were gathered up and buried in a plot just north of the fort. In 1870 they were dug up and reinterred in a national cemetery plot west of town, and a monument was erected in honor of all the Federal soldiers who died at Baxter Springs on October 6, 1863.

Monument to soldiers killed at Baxter Springs. *Photo by the author.*

After spending the winter of 1863-64 in Texas, Quantrill again passed through the southwest Missouri area on his way back to his old stomping grounds in the northern part of the state. His command had disintegrated in Texas, and he led just eighty to a hundred men as he passed near Neosho on the 18th of May. His reduced numbers didn't deter the Rebel chieftain from seeking redress for his ill-fated assault on Lamar a year and a half earlier. At daybreak on the 20th the guerrillas slammed into the town a second

104

time, attacking a forty to fifty-man garrison that included about an equal number of civilians and Enrolled Missouri Militia. Many of the Federals, who had just risen and were preparing breakfast or feeding their horses, scattered at the first sign of the sudden attack, but about ten managed to get behind the walls of the burned out courthouse, where the arms and ammunition were stored.

Quantrill's advance had charged to within about fifty yards when the small group of defenders fired a volley that caused the Rebels to fall back to the cover of buildings. From their sheltered position the guerrillas yelled for the Federals to surrender, promising them fair treatment. The militia, rightly suspecting the desperate character of their enemy, refused. Better to fight to the death than to cooperate and be rewarded with a bullet through the head.

When Quantrill realized his ploy was not going to work, he formed his entire force in a line and charged the fortress again. This time the guerrillas got to within forty yards before another well-aimed volley from the besieged Federals dropped several riders from the saddle and stopped the remainder in their tracks. The bushwhackers pulled their wounded from the courtyard and dropped back a second time.

Presently the stubborn Rebels launched still another assault, but when it, too, was repelled, they retired from the field in frustration, carrying off an undetermined number of their dead and wounded. The Federals lost but one man in the skirmish, a civilian named Underwood who was killed on the street at the onset of the attack before he was able to get inside the courthouse walls. They also had several horses killed.[32]

(Shortly after this episode, the local militia temporarily left Lamar, leaving only women and children in town, and on May 29 Henry Taylor, guerrilla leader from Vernon County, dashed into the defenseless village and burned ten houses.)[33]

Quantrill spent the summer and fall of 1864 holed up in Howard County, Missouri, in relative inactivity. Around Christmas of 1864 he rallied about forty guerrillas and led them east on a mission that was as mysterious as the man himself. Popular legend says he was on his way to Washington to assassinate the president. Former guerrillas suggested that he wanted to get his men close to General Lee so that they would be treated as prisoners of war when they surrendered.[34] More likely he was simply determined to hold out to the very end, and he wanted to get away from Missouri, where increased Federal vigilance had made bushwhacking a dangerous pastime. Quantrill was mortally wounded by Federal guerrillas in Kentucky on May 10, 1865, a month after Lee's surrender to Grant, and the guerrilla chieftain died twenty-seven days later in a Louisville hospital.

8
Jo Shelby and the
1863 Raid into Missouri

Joseph Orville Shelby, a Kentucky-born aristocrat, moved to Missouri as a young man, settling finally in Waverly on the Missouri River, where he established a rope factory and became a prosperous planter. A supporter of slavery, he raised and led a company of pro-Southern forces during the Kansas-Missouri border conflict that arose over the issue of Kansas statehood during the late 1850s.

In 1861 at the beginning of the Civil War, the thirty-year-old Shelby declined a commission in the Union Army from his cousin, Congressman Frank P. Blair, Jr., and became instead captain of a cavalry unit in Price's Missouri State Guard. "Jo" Shelby, as he was familiarly known, fought in every important campaign in Missouri and Arkansas during the first year of the war, including Carthage, Wilson's Creek, Lexington, and Pea Ridge.[1]

During the summer of 1862 he went on a recruiting expedition to the Missouri River, raised 1,000 men in four days at his hometown of Waverly, and was rewarded with a Confederate colonel's commission and command of a brigade upon his return south in early September. Major General Thomas Hindman mustered the recruits into service as the Fourth Missouri Cavalry and organized Shelby's Missouri Brigade. In addition to the Fourth, the 2,500-man command included Colonel Upton Hays's Twelfth Missouri Cavalry, Colonel John Coffee's Sixth Missouri Cavalry, and Captain Joseph Bledsoe's artillery battery. The brigade was assigned to General Marmaduke's cavalry division.

In late September Shelby fought at Newtonia. (Colonel Hays was killed in a skirmish leading up to the main battle.) Shelby's command was heavily engaged at Cane Hill in November and also participated in the Battle of Prairie Grove in early December, earning the nickname the "Iron Brigade" for its rugged and determined fighting. After Prairie Grove, the Confederate Army of the Trans-Mississippi Department was re-organized, and Shelby's brigade was once again assigned to Marmaduke's division. The brigade consisted of Bledsoe's artillery battery and cavalry regiments under Colonel B. Frank Gordon (Shelby's regiment), B.G. Jeans (who had succeeded to command of Hays's unit), and Gideon W. Thompson (who had taken over Coffee's regiment after Coffee was arrested).

In early January 1863, Shelby participated in Marmaduke's raid on Springfield, and during the spring, he covered the general's retreat from eastern Missouri. In July of that year, Shelby was wounded in the Battle of Helena, Arkansas, but quickly recovered and in September launched what would become the longest cavalry raid of the Civil War, a 1,500-mile march that took him from Arkadelphia, Arkansas, to the Missouri River and back to Arkansas.

Shelby set out from Arkadelphia on the 22nd of September with detachments from his three regiments, the total force numbering about 600. Although the Union Army had previously driven the Confederates well south of the Arkansas River, the Federals did not yet occupy Arkansas in any considerable numbers, and Shelby passed to the northwest corner of the state with little resistance. Near Bentonville on the last day of September, he was reinforced by 200 men under Colonel D.C. Hunter of Vernon County. On October 3 the Rebels marched to Pineville, where in the colorful words of Shelby's adjutant and chief of staff, Major John N. Edwards, "Missouri breezes blew and Missouri skies looked down upon us."[2]

At Pineville, Shelby was joined by another 400 men under Colonel Coffee, who had been harassing Union targets and keeping Federal troops in Southwest Missouri busy chasing after him all summer. At daylight on the 4th, the Confederate brigade, with now upwards of 1,200 men, started for Neosho, where, according to Edwards, who composed all of Shelby's battlefield reports after the fall of 1862, "there were 300 Federal cavalry stationed—a terror to the country, the insulters of unprotected women, and the murderers of old and infirm men." As he approached the town, Shelby deployed his forces in several directions in order to surround the enemy.[3]

In fact, the number of Federals at Neosho was considerably less than Shelby's estimate. At mid-morning, Captain Henry V. Stall of the Sixth Missouri Militia Cavalry had departed with a wagon train on the Newtonia road, leaving thirty men in Neosho to receive Captain Charles B. McAfee of the same regiment, who was expected later in the day. Just east of town Captain Stall met Captain McAfee on his way to Pineville with about 130 men to join Major Austin A. King, also of the Sixth Cavalry, in pursuit of Coffee, who was rumored to be concentrating his forces in that area. After passing McAfee, Captain Stall skirmished briefly with a detachment of Shelby's force but managed to get his train out of the Neosho area with just two men wounded.

Colonel Jo Shelby led a raid through Missouri in the fall of 1863. *Author's collection.*

Meanwhile, Captain McAfee entered Neosho about 11:00 a.m. and, after learning nothing of the whereabouts of Major King, started toward Pineville in search of him. About a mile or two outside Neosho, McAfee came upon Coffee's ragtag outfit, which briefly formed in a line but quickly fell back through the woods and started in the direction of the town. McAfee sent messengers along the road back to Neosho to warn the guard left there of the Rebel threat, while he started back to town in an indirect route with the rest of his command.

Approaching from opposite directions, the Federals and Confederates reached Neosho at the same time and opened fire on each other. The Rebels dropped back but quickly came up again as the several bodies of Shelby's cavalry converged on the town from different directions. McAfee promptly took shelter in the brick courthouse, which was pierced with holes for small arms, and again drove the enemy back. The Federals remained behind their fortress for about an hour and a half, exchanging fire with the invaders. According to Shelby (i.e. Major Edwards), the barricaded Yankees "kept up a hot fire upon our advancing columns..., and the Federals were already beginning to laugh at the fire of my skirmishers, when I ordered my cannon into position...."[4]

Shelby then sent four balls smashing through the walls of the brick building. Hoisting a white flag of truce, he demanded the immediate and unconditional surrender of the Federals in the courthouse. McAfee agreed only on the condition that all the Federals, including the few Enrolled Missouri Militia garrisoned at the courthouse, be treated as prisoners of war. Shelby at first objected, according to McAfee's report of October 10, "refusing to treat Enrolled Missouri Militia as prisoners of war." After additional parleying, including a threat from Shelby to shell the town, McAfee agreed to an immediate surrender on the courthouse grounds, and the Rebel commander agreed to treat all captives as prisoners of war.[5]

McAfee surrendered his command, which, including the Enrolled Militia and a few private citizens, totaled about 180 men. Shelby took their names and paroled them upon their sworn promise not to take up arms against the Confederate States of America until such time as an exchange of prisoners might be duly arranged. He then confiscated all of the Federal horses, arms, wagons, and provisions before setting out northeast in the direction of Sarcoxie, tarrying in Neosho "only long enough to distribute the arms and ammunition."[6]

Captain McAfee reported two men killed and two wounded in the fight with Shelby. He also said that two Enrolled Missouri Militia were killed by Coffee's men after they had been paroled. McAfee put the enemy loss at five killed and nine wounded.

Shelby left Neosho about four in the afternoon and rested for five hours on Jones Creek, where his command took supper. The next day, according to his report, he "passed through the blackened and desolated town of Sarcoxie, whose bare and fire-scarred chimneys point with skeleton fingers to heaven for vengeance."[7]

From Sarcoxie the Confederates pushed due north to Bower's Mill, which Shelby considered "a notorious pest spot for the militia."[8] After dispersing a detachment of seventeen men under Captain T.J. Stemmons, Shelby put the town to the torch. According to his report, the community "was sacked and then swept from the face of the earth, to pollute it no more forever...."[9]

Leaving Bower's Mill, the Rebels struck northeast toward Greenfield and camped on the evening of October 5th about eighteen miles from the town.

Union forces concentrated at Newtonia for the chase after Shelby. The commands of Colonel John D. Allen of the Seventh Provisional Enrolled Militia, Major Edward B. Eno of the Eighth Missouri State Militia Cavalry, and Major King of the Sixth Missouri State Militia Cavalry arrived there early on the morning of the 5th, making a total force of about 550 men. The Federals had to wait all day, though, for food supplies to arrive from Cassville. By the time they set out on Shelby's trail that evening, they were more than twenty-four hours behind the Confederates.

Meanwhile, Colonel John Edwards, temporarily in command at Springfield in the absence of General McNeil, learned of the Rebel incursion and sent word to Majors Eno and King to meet him at Greenfield, where Shelby was thought to be headed. Edwards set out from Springfield with 150 men and three artillery pieces, hoping to cut the invaders off at the Dade county seat.

In the early morning hours of October 6, Shelby advanced on Greenfield and by daylight had the town surrounded. Major Wick Morgan, commanding a company of the Seventh Provisional Enrolled Missouri Militia at Greenfield, chose to abandon the town rather than try to make a stand against the superior Confederate force. According to his report written at 11:00 a.m. the same day, Morgan "managed to get (his) men in the brush all safe."[10]

Shelby complained that "the nest was there, and warm, but the birds had flown." He added, however, that his advance did skirmish briefly with Morgan's rear, "killing some and capturing some."[11] Morgan made no mention of any such engagement or of any casualties, although thirty of his men out on patrol had not yet come in at the time of his report.

After scattering the militia, Shelby took possession of the town, confiscating the contents of several stores and capturing a quantity of arms and ammunition. He also set fire to the courthouse, or, as he told General Marmaduke in his report of November 16, "destroyed a strong fort."

Leaving Greenfield, the Confederates rode north to Stockton, arriving about 3:00 p.m., and also burned the courthouse there after driving out a few militia. They camped the night of the 6th ten miles north of Stockton. At Humansville the next day a detachment of ten Rebels dashed up to Osceola and skirmished with Federal militia there before rejoining the main Rebel march at Warsaw.

Union reports during Shelby's march north put his strength at 1,200 to 1,500 men when the Confederates first entered Missouri, but by the time they reached Greenfield, the estimated range had risen to 1,500-2,000. One Federal officer suggested as many as 4,000. The latter was an obvious exaggeration, but the prevailing Union estimate was probably quite accurate, because Shelby was picking up recruits and gathering in small guerrilla bands all along the way.

The Rebel procession formed a motley cavalcade, with some men dressed in ragged Confederate gray, some wearing drab civilian attire, some sporting confiscated Federal uniforms, and nearly all bedecked with flaming sumac plumes in their hats to identify themselves. To Southern sympathizers, though, Shelby's march through Missouri was a grand and welcome spectacle, and many flocked to the Iron Brigade in thirst of redemption.

Union officials, on the other hand, viewed the raiders with varying degrees of contempt. Major Emory S. Foster of the Seventh Missouri State Militia Cavalry, for example, complained in an October 8th letter from Warsaw, "Fifty of these whelps go in advance with a Federal flag and Federal clothing."[12] Union officers considered many of the men under Shelby, in particular Coffee and his regiment, to be guerrillas and marauders.

Loyal citizens, meanwhile, greeted the invasion with alarm. Shelby's report describes the situation among the civilian population along one segment of his route north of Stockton:

> All along this road the inhabitants had their household furniture taken from their houses, and waiting in silence and in sorrow for us to apply the torch, it having been represented to them that my command was laying the country waste, as though God had sent the whirlwind and the storm to drive back the laws of nature and desolate the land with fire, pestilence, and famine. On this route every house belonging to a Southern family has been burned, and the family as effectually destroyed as if the waves of the Dead Sea had rolled over them with their dread monotony.[13]

At Greenfield on the morning of October 7, Colonel Edwards formed a junction with Majors Eno and King and 600 Enrolled Missouri Militia under General C.B. Holland. They were still twenty-four hours behind Shelby, but Edwards nevertheless set out in pursuit of the raiders and followed them as far as Hickory County before receiving word from General John Schofield, commanding the Department of Missouri, to stay south of the Osage River with the expectation that Shelby would soon be driven back from the central part of the state.

Passing rapidly through southwest Missouri into the central part of the state, Shelby did not encounter significant Federal resistance until he reached Warsaw in Benton County, where he met a force of Federals drawn up in a line to contest his crossing of the Osage. He managed to cross without difficulty, but the rest of his march through Missouri was hounded at every turn. For the next four days he kept up a running fight, skirmishing with the enemy each day and sometimes more than once a day as he made his way to the Missouri River. Federals pressed him from all directions, and when one force tired, another promptly took up the chase.

At Marshall the Federal pursuit caught up to him on the 13th, and he was forced to make a stand against superior numbers. After a hard fight of several hours, he was able to disengage, but his command became divided during the escape, as Hunter's regiment moved off to the southeast while Shelby with the main body retired in a westerly direction. The pursuit continued, and it was so hot that

Shelby was forced to abandon much of the plunder he had taken since entering the state. Finally at Waverly, rather than be slowed by his train, he dumped his wagons into the Missouri River "where they were safe from all capture."[14]

Both Shelby and Hunter now turned south in an all-out flight for Arkansas. According to Union brigadier general E.B. Brown, commanding the District of Central Missouri, the enemy was "running like wild hogs."[15]

Brigadier General Thomas Ewing, Jr., commander of the District of the Border, overtook Shelby at sundown on October 14 in Bates County about fifteen miles east of Butler and skirmished with the Confederate rear, "killing one and capturing several," according to the general's report written immediately following the incident.[16] While the Federals paused during the night for food and rest, though, Shelby pushed on, again breaking contact with his pursuers.

Ewing took up the chase the next morning but found only exhausted animals left by the side of the road lining the trail of Shelby's retreat, as one horse after another broke down from the Rebels' relentless ride. Fortunately for the Confederates, they had captured numerous horses during their raid so that, as soon as one animal faltered, they replaced it with a fresh mount.

Ewing failed to catch up with the Rebels until he reached Carthage on the early morning of the 18th. Here he captured a detachment of thirty Confederates under Major J.F. Pickler, who had been allowed by Shelby the previous evening to spend the night in town on a foraging expedition because many of Pickler's men were from the area. Shelby, with the main body of troops, was camped at the Kendrick place not far outside town and drew off without an engagement at the first sign of the Federals' approach, his rear skirmishing just briefly with Ewing's advance before the exhausted Union troops stopped to rest.

From Carthage, Shelby marched southeast toward Sarcoxie and through the corners of Newton and Lawrence counties. He then headed straight south through Barry County and crossed the Wire Road (Springfield to Fayetteville Road) southwest of Cassville. Continuing into Arkansas, he was closely pursued by General McNeil, who had struck his trail at Sarcoxie twelve hours behind him.

Shelby camped at the Kendrick place during his retreat to Arkansas. *Photo by the author.*

.As Shelby passed south through the western-most tier of Missouri counties, the force under Hunter that had gotten separated from the main command at Marshall paralleled Shelby's retreat in the next tier of counties to the east. Crossing the Osage River below Warsaw, Hunter was hotly pursued by Major King, commanding detachments of the Sixth and Eighth regiments of the Missouri State Militia Cavalry. North of Humansville on October 16, King had a running fight with Hunter's rear guard, killing three Rebels and capturing the last of the three pieces of artillery the Confederates had brought to Missouri, along with forty rounds of ammunition. King continued the pursuit to Stockton, where he called it off on account of darkness.

However, Brigadier General Holland, commanding the Enrolled Militia in southwest Missouri, kept up the chase through the night and got in front of Hunter at Greenfield. Upon discovering the place occupied by militia, Hunter skirted the town through the woods and continued south. Northeast of Mount Vernon he skirmished with a detachment of General Holland's militia under Major Roswell K. Hart. The militia, though, scarcely slowed the Rebel retreat, and Hunter soon passed out of the state into Arkansas, where he reunited with Shelby on October 20 on the Little Osage.

Marching leisurely from that point, Shelby rejoined his division under General Marmaduke near Washington, Arkansas, on November 3.

A summary statement near the end of Shelby's official report offers an interesting Southern perspective on the conditions the Rebels witnessed during their expedition through Missouri:

> I have traveled 1,500 miles, and found the people of Missouri, as a mass, true to the South and her institutions, yet needing the strong presence of a Confederate army to make them volunteer. The southern, southwestern, and some of the middle counties of Missouri are completely desolated. In many places for 40 miles not a single habitation is to be found, for on the road we met delicate females fleeing southward, driving ox teams, barefooted, ragged, and suffering for even bread.[17]

Shelby's recapitulation of his campaign shows 600 Federals killed and wounded and only 150 killed and wounded on the Confederate side.[18] A similar report from the Union side summarizing Shelby's entire raid is unavailable, but, judging from Federal accounts of individual actions and skirmishes throughout the incursion, one can safely say that such a recapitulation would show a much different result.

If Shelby's raid accomplished anything significant, it is not revealed by an examination of the number of enemy killed or the amount of property destroyed. The strategic significance of the incursion is also dubious. Some have suggested that the raid kept Union troops occupied defending Missouri, thus delaying for a couple of weeks their being sent to reinforce the Federal army east of the Mississippi, but the fact is most of the Union soldiers who opposed Shelby were Missouri militia who were unavailable for duty elsewhere.

10
The Second Tier of Counties and the Affair at Germantown

Because of lingering bitterness over the border conflict with Kansas during the mid to late 1850s, Missouri citizens living near the state line tended to be more sympathetic to the Southern cause and more resistant to Union forces in their state during the Civil War than did people residing farther east. (The strong pro-Southern sentiment that existed along the Missouri River in the central part of the state was an obvious exception to the general rule.) Consequently, counties like St. Clair and Cedar didn't, for the most part, experience the degree of violence and conflict that counties such as Vernon and Bates did. However, no area of Missouri was immune to the bitter guerrilla warfare that gripped the state, and the second tier of counties witnessed its share of skirmishes and incidents. In fact, early in the war the second tier of counties to the east saw as much activity as the border counties.

On July 4, 1861, the day before Governor Jackson's Missouri State Guard and Colonel Sigel's Federals met at Carthage, a combined force of army regulars and Kansas volunteers, numbering 2,000-3,000, under Major Samuel D. Sturgis marched into Clinton in Henry County. Sturgis was on his way to hook up with General Lyon, who was headed south from Jefferson City. Although many local Southern sympathizers of fighting age had gone south with Governor Jackson, the arriving Union force still found Clinton "pretty much given over to rebellion," according to one newspaper report. It was Independence Day, but the town had "abolished the great anniversary, Yankee Doodle, and the Stars and Stripes, the American Eagle, and all other National institutions." These, however, were promptly and "fittingly reinstated by the army of the Union."[1]

Some of the Kansas volunteers celebrated the Fourth of July by getting rip-roaring drunk. A local man "rolled out a large keg of mean whiskey" and invited everybody to take a drink. A few of the men drank to excess and started committing minor depredations like stealing chickens and vegetables from area citizens. The offenders were quickly apprehended and brought before Major Sturgis, who ordered them flogged by some of his regulars. The next day, eight soldiers and one teamster were tied to a cannon, one after another, and given fifty lashes each on the bare back with a teamster's black-snake whip. The harsh punishment caused a minor mutiny among the Kansas volunteers, some of whom threatened to kill Sturgis, and a Union newspaper questioned why U.S. soldiers were dealt with so severely for their indiscretions while men who were in open rebellion against the government were let off by simply taking an oath.[2]

Shortly after the flogging incident, the Union soldiers marched to Osceola in St. Clair County, where they were to be joined by Lyon and then proceed to Springfield. However, the second tier of counties continued to see a good deal of activity throughout the summer and fall of 1861. Osceola was, of course, the site of Jim Lane's infamous raid in late September. Then during late November and early December, General Price established a recruiting camp and temporary headquarters in the Osceola area after his army had fallen back from Lexington to southwest Missouri. On November 27, 1861, Brigadier General William T. Sherman (who gained fame later in the war during his march through Georgia), complained from his Sedalia headquarters that the country around Osceola was "full of returned secessionists, who are driving out all Union men."[3]

Near the end of 1861, Price moved his headquarters to Springfield, and recruits from the northern part of the state were still pouring in early the next year when he was forced to relinquish his hold on southwest Missouri and retreat to Arkansas. Many of the prospective Rebel recruits, unable to get south in time to link up with Price, gathered in the Henry County area, "producing a reign of terror and rendering it impossible for the militia to organize for their own defense."[4]

In response to the situation, Major General Henry W. Halleck, commanding the Department of the Missouri, ordered troops to Clinton in mid-March of 1862 to break up the marauding bands. Colonel Fitz Henry Warren and the First Iowa Cavalry arrived on March 18, and Colonel Warren promptly sent out scouting parties in two separate directions. One detachment under Captain William H. Ankeny scoured the country southeast of Clinton and skirmished with a band of Rebels southeast of Leesville near the Henry-Benton county line. The Federals reported killing "two of the worst Rebels, Swykiffer and John Raftre, both desperate characters." They also wounded one man, captured ten, and confiscated several guns and horses. Union officials placed their own loss at four men wounded and one horse killed.[5]

A few days later, on March 24, Warren took 200 hundred men south into St. Clair County. Marching up the Osage River, the Federals had a brisk skirmish with a band of guerrillas in the hills near Monegaw Springs. Warren reported two Rebels wounded fatally and three severely, while three Union soldiers were slightly wounded. The colonel arrived back at Clinton on March 27, and a detachment that he'd left on the Osage near the mouth of Salt Creek came in the next day with sixteen prisoners, one of whom was badly wounded. On March 30, another detachment skirmished near Clinton with a band of Rebels, killing one, wounding seven, and capturing nineteen more prisoners. By the end of March, the First Iowa had rounded up over a hundred prisoners during the previous two weeks, although many of them were released on bond. The Federal troops had effectually accomplished what they'd been sent to Henry County to do—break up the bands around Clinton. Colonel Warren soon moved his headquarters to Butler, and the focus of Federal efforts in the region shifted to Bates County, where Rebel leader Sidney Jackman was operating.[6]

Minor skirmishing continued sporadically, however, in the area of Henry and St. Clair counties throughout the spring and summer of 1862. On April 11, Lieutenant Colonel Charles E. Moss, recently stationed at Osceola, left his headquarters with eighty men of the First Iowa Cavalry and forty of the Twenty-sixth Indiana Infantry to break up a reported band of 200 Rebels under Major Elbert S. Feaster of the Missouri State Guard. A Benton County resident, Feaster was recruiting in his home territory for the purpose of joining the Confederacy. He and his men were gathered fifteen to twenty miles northeast of Osceola on Hoyle's Creek at a place called Shiloh Camp.[7]

After marching down the Osage River for several miles, Moss sent the infantry detachment across the hills to a point that his cavalry could only reach by a more circuitous route. About the time Moss started with the cavalry toward Shiloh, a cold rain set in, forcing most of the Rebels to abandon their camp and seek shelter in homes and other buildings. When the Federals found Feaster and about thirty guerrillas at a nearby house, the advance guard of sixteen soldiers attacked immediately, while the main body of troops took up a position between the house and the supposed Rebel camp to prevent the men in the house from either retreating to the camp or receiving reinforcements from it. Moss reported six Rebels killed in the attack, four wounded and seven taken prisoner, and he claimed the Union had just two men injured when their horses fell. After the skirmish, Moss returned to Osceola and sent orders to the infantry to return as well. When the Indiana troops reached Osceola the next day, they brought in one prisoner and reported they'd killed one guerrilla and wounded three others.[8]

Captain William E. Leffingwell of the First Iowa Cavalry replaced Lieutenant Colonel Moss in command of the post at Osceola on April 24, 1862. The next day, Leffingwell sent a detachment of fifty men to break up a band of guerrillas reportedly camped near Monegaw Springs. The Federals found seventeen Rebels gathered in the vicinity, ten on the north side of the Osage River and seven on the south. The first soldiers on the scene, a squad of seven, immediately attacked the Rebels on the north side, killing one, wounding one, and capturing the remaining eight, with no loss on the Union side. The Federals also fired across the river at the seven guerrillas on the south side and managed to shoot one Rebel horse as the bushwhackers made their escape.[9]

The skirmish at Monegaw Springs, however, was a relatively isolated incident, as Leffingwell's April 28 report of the affair suggests. The captain said the daily scouts he had been sending out almost always returned without having discovered any enemy. "The whole country around us is comparatively quiety."[10]

It was a month and a half later before Leffingwell had occasion to take up his pen again to describe hostilities. One June 11, a detachment he had sent out from Osceola skirmished with and dispersed a band of Rebels near Taberville on the Osage River in western St. Clair County. The Federals killed three men, wounded four, and captured five in the affray, while the only reported Union loss was an injury sustained by a private who had his wrist dislocated during a hand-to-hand fight with a guerrilla whom he ultimately killed. According to Leffingwell, the Rebels were commanded by Upton Hays, who had his shoulder broken and was taken prisoner during the skirmish. However, the report is dubious, since Hays was active very shortly after this incident. If he was captured on June 11, he must have escaped or been released almost immediately, and if he was seriously injured, as Leffingwell thought, he must have made a very speedy recovery.[11]

On July 30, 1862, four bushwhackers killed a man named James Scott, "an old and most estimable citizen" of Henry County. Scott, who lived about halfway between Clinton and Calhoun, was out in his field plowing when the "armed devils" rode up to the fence and two of them opened fire, killing him instantly. Some of the First Iowa troops were fired on from the brush the same day and in the same general neighborhood. In reporting the incidents to a St. Louis newspaper, a local correspondent suggested that the recent enrollment order, issued on July 22, which required all able-bodied men in Missouri to report for militia duty, was creating intense excitement among citizens in the Henry County area (as elsewhere) and causing many men to take to the brush to avoid the enrollment. "We are to have the worst of trouble here," the correspondent predicted, "and plenty of it—guerrilla war to the death."[12]

As if on cue, a detachment of 135 troops from the First Iowa under Captains Joseph W. Caldwell and Herman H. Heath came upon a large body of guerrillas on Clear Creek in the southwest corner of St. Clair County on August 2, the same day the local correspondent's ominous forecast was printed in the St. Louis newspaper. Captain Caldwell advanced directly toward the Rebels, who were strongly posted at the edge of some timber and obscured by brush. Meanwhile, Captain Heath began a flanking movement and, in so doing, according to Colonel Warren, "encountered an ambush and had to run the gauntlet of their entire line. Not a man was visible, and the whole front blazed with the flash of fire." Four Federal soldiers were killed and nine others, including Captain Heath, were wounded during the officer's "experiment of running a flank along a double line of shot-guns and Minie muskets at thirty yards." Despite the unfavorable outcome of the "experiment," Colonel Warren praised Heath for his boldness, claiming his charge was "of the 'Six hundred' style."[13]

While Heath was conducting his trial run, Captain Caldwell dismounted sixty men, took cover behind a rail fence, and engaged the Rebels with a lively fire. Caldwell maintained his position until a firing in his rear aroused his concern. After falling back to check on his horses and the safety of his rear, he moved up for another attack, but, in the meantime, the Rebels had dispersed, taking their dead and wounded with them. Colonel Warren reported the Federal loss during Caldwell's exchange with the guerrillas at two men killed and three wounded. He claimed that a Rebel named Clarey, who was taken prisoner during the action, confessed to a guerrilla loss of eleven killed and eighteen wounded. The prisoner supposedly said to one of the Federals with whom he was acquainted, "You cut us up like hell."[14]

Clarey was credited with having protected the lives of some wounded and captured Federals prior to being captured himself, and no doubt he commanded a certain amount of sympathy among his captors. He was placed in a ball and chain, but by the time of Colonel Warren's report two days after the skirmish, he had already "escaped" by sawing off a rivet. The colonel declined to offer an explanation as to how Clarey so readily came by a tool capable of sawing off a steel rivet.[15]

Colonel Warren closed his report of the Clear Creek skirmish with what was, at this comparatively early stage of the Civil War when many thought compromise still possible, a rare insight into the unforgiving nature of the guerrilla conflict in Missouri. "It is to be a war of extermination," he declared. "There is no half-way house and no neutral position. We are to be driven out and annihilated or they are. It is an inveterate, malignant hatred, which will last to the end of life."[16]

On September 20, 1862, the Iowa troops left Clinton for Springfield, leaving the Henry County area in the hands of the recently organized Enrolled Missouri Militia. The local militia promptly marched to Calhoun for the purpose of transporting to Sedalia some prisoners who had been left at the former place by the First Iowa. Then on the evening of September 21, a band of about fifty or sixty guerrillas, having apparently been apprised of the Union movements, swept into Clinton and took possession of the town that the Federals had abandoned the day before. The Rebels, led by one Teague of Cass County and Richard J. DeJarnett of Bates County, made a quick search for militia or other armed men and then proceeded to the residence of Judge Jerald G. Dorman, a strong Union man and proprietor of a local store. The guerrillas told Dorman they'd come to requisition his goods and he could either come with them, hand over his key to the store, or oblige them to break the door down. "The Judge, being a retail dealer, thought proper to witness this wholesale distribution of his goods," remarked a correspondent to a St. Louis newspaper, "and accompanied them to his store."[17]

The Rebels, who had come prepared with sacks, loaded up on sugar, coffee, slat, and everything else they could haul off. While they were still stacking up and dividing the goods, two couples who lived near the store came out and "begged them to desist." The local residents said that the judge was a Union man but that he had been very considerate of Southern men and their families, having supplied the families with food and other necessities. The two ladies appealed to the Rebels as "Southern gentlemen" to take only what they actually needed and to leave the rest for others, but the guerrillas were unrelenting, and according to the local correspondent, "did not much increase these ladies' exalted opinion of the "Southern chivalry."[18]

As soon as news of the raid on Clinton reached Calhoun, sixty men of the Henry County Enrolled Missouri Militia under Captain William Weaver and thirty men of the Bates County Enrolled Missouri Militia under Lieutenant Ava Page set out in pursuit of the guerrillas. After a futile twenty-four-mile chase, the militiamen stopped about ten miles north of Clinton on the morning of September 23 to feed and rest themselves and their horses. The command was divided, with a portion under Captain Weaver going to a nearby house and the remainder under Lieutenant Page retiring to a separate residence. As Weaver's men were approaching the barn and stables to feed their horses, a party of guerrillas suddenly rushed out from the surrounding brush and opened fire, wounding three of the Federals severely and two slightly. The militia managed to return fire, killing three of the bushwhackers and driving the rest back into the brush. Weaver, however, declined to pursue them because a larger body of guerrillas were thought to be concealed deeper in the woods. Upon inspection, one of the dead Rebels, a man named Wash Hampton, was found dressed in a new pair of boots and a new shirt that had been taken from Judge Dorman's store, suggesting that the guerrillas encountered by the militia were almost certainly the same party that had raided Clinton.[19]

Although the counties directly south of Henry and St. Clair tended to be relatively calmer than both their western and their northern neighbors during the Civil War, isolated skirmishes and incidents occasionally erupted in Cedar, Dade, and Lawrence. Winding through western Dade County, northeastern Barton County, and southwestern Cedar County, Horse Creek served as a frequent rendezvous for guerrillas and was a particularly troublesome spot for Federal authorities. One Union observer called the area a "'Hell's half acre' of secession."[20]

In late November of 1862, a scout of twenty-five men from the Fourth Missouri State Militia Cavalry came into the area to try to break up a nest of Rebels that had been harbored throughout the fall by the families living on Horse Creek. At the community of White Hare, twenty men of the Cedar County Enrolled Missouri Militia joined the Federals as guides, "the only purpose in God's world that these men serve," remarked an observer from Greenfield a few days later. Striking Horse Creek west of White Hare, the scouting party proceeded up the creek and soon discovered a band of Rebels under a Captain Thomas at the edge of a wide-open prairie. "Then commenced the pursuit," said the Greenfield correspondent, "for the Rebels, as soon as the blue coats fell upon their sight, broke for 'tall timber,' and away went the scouts in hot chase, pell-mell, helter-skelter, after them."[21]

One of the cavalrymen, Captain Joe Parks, outraced the other pursuers and soon overtook the "flying Rebels." Parks ordered a straggling guerrilla to halt, informing him that he was a prisoner, and then resumed the chase after the next Rebel. This was repeated until the Federal captain caught up with a lieutenant in General Rains's division named Jerome B. McAbee, of Henry County. When Parks ordered McAbee to surrender, the latter replied, "Shoot me and be damned." Parks attempted to oblige the request, but the hammer of his revolver landed on an empty chamber, as he had already fired out his ammunition at other guerrillas. Seeing that the Federal was out of ammunition, McAbee pulled out his own revolver and fired at Parks. When the shot missed, Parks rushed McAbee and "then began a contest of life and death between the armed rebel and the unarmed Federal officer. Capt. Joe…pitched into Mr. Rebel fist and skull.

Grappling him so close that the rebel could not use his firearms, Capt. Joe pounded away at the rebel's face...."[22]

While the combatants were still engaged in their desperate struggle, another Federal officer arrived on the scene and handed Parks a loaded revolver, and McAbee was soon dispatched with a ball through the lung and another through the head. He was the only Rebel killed during the chase, but eight others were taken prisoner. Among the captives were three Rectors of Barton County, who were considered "old offenders," and a man named James Anderson of Lafayette County.[23] (This could have been Bloody Bill Anderson's brother Jim, because the Anderson gang made its headquarters in Lafayette County during the fall and winter of 1862-1863.)

A band of guerrillas under William Gregg heading north toward Jackson County to recruit for Marmaduke's army, captured a party of about ten Enrolled Missouri Militia, including a Lieutenant Hacket, south of the Osage River near Osceola on January 17, 1863. After transporting the captives across the river by ferry, the Rebels relieved the Federals of their uniforms, weapons, and horses. The prisoners were then set free with paroles signed by "W.H. Gregg, Quantrill's Regiment, Marmaduke's Division."[24]

About the same time, John Raftre, "a guerrilla chief of some notoriety," was reported prowling about Clinton.[25] This, of course, was the same John Raftre who was supposedly killed near Leesville in March of 1862, along with the notorious Swykiffer.

On the morning of May 2, 1863, a soldier of the Seventh Cavalry Missouri State Militia named John W. Galloway, who was home on furlough, was shot and killed by a bushwhacker a few miles south of Calhoun in Henry County, Upon hearing of the incident, a detachment of militia rode out to the neighborhood where it had happened and killed a man named John Brown, who was presumed to be the guilty party, because he'd been skulking in the neighborhood for more than a month.[26]

In mid-August 1863, a Confederate recruiting officer named Charles V. Snelling was captured and brought to the post at Clinton, where Lieutenant-Colonel James H. Brown of the Enrolled Missouri Militia commanded. Considered a "notorious bushwhacker" by the Union, Snelling had led an attack on a wagon train in Johnson County around the beginning of 1862, burned the wagons, and reportedly killed a number of sick soldiers who were being escorted to Kansas City. In the summer of 1862, he had cooperated with

Upton Hays and John Brinker (later a captain in Quantrill's regiment), and he was considered "the terror of Johnson and Henry counties." Thus, Colonel Brown convened a summary court composed of a few officers of the post, and, after the tribunal found Snelling guilty, he was executed by firing squad.[27]

Just a few days after Snelling's execution, three more Rebels; Thaddeus Dunn, Robert Marshall, and a boy named Robbins; were captured south of Leesville and brought to the Clinton post. Dunn and Marshall, like Snelling, were promptly executed, while Robbins was spared because of his youth.

On September 4, 1863, a band of guerrillas under the "notorious Rafter" dashed into Quincy just across the St. Clair line in Hickory County and immediately started shooting up the place. Blazing away at some men who were sitting in front of a store, the Rebels killed one citizen. Next they turned their attention to four soldiers of the Eighteenth Iowa Volunteers who had arrived on a stagecoach moments before and taken shelter in a house. The guerrillas followed them to an upstairs room and took them prisoner. The raiders then plundered the businesses and were in the act of setting fire to the buildings when a party of the Eighth Missouri State Militia Cavalry rode into town and opened fire, scattering the bushwhackers and recapturing much of the supplies taken from the town. Killed in the skirmish was the guerrilla leader, John Raftre, and, unlike the previous year, this time he stayed dead. His sidekicks, however, made off with the four Iowa soldiers they'd captured, and they killed the prisoners several miles outside town.[28]

On September 11, 1863, three weeks after the infamous sacking of Lawrence, a note, purported to be from Quantrill, was received by Lieutenant John A. Devinney at Clinton threatening to burn the town and kill all the citizens if the militia stationed there and all the male citizens did not vacate the place within three days. September 14 passed without incident, however; so the note might have been a mere hoax.[29]

On October 18, 1863, a party of the Fifth Provisional Regiment of the Enrolled Missouri Militia was sent out from Clinton to the Honey Creek vicinity northwest of town "to kill some bushwhackers and house robbers who have been for months a terror to the people in that part of the country." The next day, the militiamen came upon four guerrillas just as they were finishing dinner at a residence in the neighborhood, attacked them, and, true to orders, killed all four of them."[30]

One of the more interesting episodes of the Civil War in Henry County area occurred in March of 1864. On the evening of the 26th, a party of guerrillas came into Deepwater Township and started "menacing the citizens and committing the most outrageous acts of plunder." A man named Short (probably William D. Short) hurried to the headquarters of Captain Joseph H. Little of the First Missouri State Militia Cavalry, camped at Germantown, to report the situation, and Little promptly dispatched a detachment under Sergeant John W. Barkley to the vicinity.[31]

When he arrived on the scene around midnight, Barkley learned that, after Short's departure, another citizen of the neighborhood, Archibald Colson, had shot and severely wounded one of the bushwhackers and that they had fled the area, taking the injured man with them. The Federals immediately set out in pursuit and soon caught up with the Rebels, whose flight was hindered by the condition of their wounded comrade. Three of the guerrillas, including the wounded man, were posted in a house of a man named Matthew Dunn, and when Barkley ordered them to surrender, the leader, who gave his name as A.D. Jones of the Confederate States Army, answered with a defiant shout and a burst of gunfire.[32]

As the Federals returned fire, the rest of the guerrillas, who had been plundering in the neighborhood, came charging up to the house, firing and yelling, and imploring their comrades inside the house to make a break for it. The leader attempted to do so, but, when he opened the door, the Federals fired a volley at him and he retreated into the house. The two sides then kept up a sporadic exchange of fire throughout the night.[33]

Around daylight, the guerrilla leader finally offered to surrender if he and his comrades would be treated as prisoners of war. Sergeant Barkley replied that they would be treated as such if they could prove themselves Confederate soldiers but that, if they were bushwhackers, they would have to suffer the consequences. The Rebel leader accepted this condition after being assured that he and his men would receive a fair trial.[34]

The Rebels emerged from the house wearing Federal overcoats and carrying U.S. Remington revolvers. They were taken back to the Federal camp at Germantown and placed under a heavy guard. When offered food, the guerrilla leader ate ravenously, but the other uninjured man, who gave his name as Ratliff, refused to eat. Neither man "would give any truthful answer to any question asked them."[35]

About three hours later, after several robbery victims from the township arrived and identified some property that Sergeant Barkley had confiscated from the guerrillas, Captain Little ordered a drumhead court martial of the two uninjured Rebels, with Barkley and four officers composing the tribunal. The civilian witnesses identified the two men as part of a band that had committed several outrages the previous winter. The guerrilla leader at first offered a "shrewd defense," but, trapped in a lie, he grew bold and said, "If I have to die, I've paid for my life nine times."[36]

The two Rebels were convicted, and at ten a.m. Captain Little ordered them executed. The condemned men were allowed to write letters and send money and valuable to their friends, and they were then taken before the firing squad. At the last moment, the guerrilla leader proclaimed his true identity, revealing that he was "the notorious Benton Gann, of Lafayette County, who has long commanded a marauding band on the border." His sullen sidekick proved to be "George Herold, of Cass County, one of Gann's men." The guerrillas still refused, however, to give any useful intelligence, and they stated that "they were not afraid to die, which boast they made good. They calmly walked to the grave, looked contemptuously on the detail assembled, said they were ready, quietly folded their arms, kneeled down, and met death with a dauntlessness worthy of a better cause."[37]

The wounded Rebel, who insisted his name was Jones (but whose real name was Alexander Clurmes), was sent to Clinton to be attended by a surgeon, although he was not expected to live. "He is one of the most desperate men I have ever seen," Captain Little allowed. "He positively refuses to give any information; scowls on those who come near him. He ought to have been executed at once, but humanity revolts at the thought of executing any one so horribly mutilated as he is at present; but, if not ordered to the contrary, I shall execute him if he recovers."[38]

Although many citizens of Henry and St. Clair counties held Southern sympathies at the beginning of the Civil War, most of these residents had been driven out by 1864, and the region was firmly in the grip of the Union. Guerrillas occasionally still came and went, but, with less grain and fewer sympathizing citizens to sustain them, they were unable to maintain an effective presence. In reporting on the state of affairs in his District of Central Missouri in the spring of 1864, Brigadier General Egbert B. Brown noted, "Henry County is sparsely populated and loyal. Bates is depopulated, and Saint Clair not much better; the inhabitants that remain in them are generally loyal."[39]

Guerrilla activity became sporadic and was mainly reduced to minor raids like the one at Calhoun in mid-June of 1864. On the evening of the 12th, a party of about twenty guerrillas dashed into the small town; burned a church, a tavern, and two homes; and robbed two stores. The Rebel leader, "Dr. Beck, a notorious character," was killed by Lieutenant Thomas Sallee of the local home guard, while three of the guards were wounded."[40]

Besides the affair at Germantown, one of the few other notable episodes of 1864 in the second tier of counties occurred in Dade County when a large party of Rebels under Pete Roberts and Kinch West dashed into the community of Melville (now Dadeville) early on the morning of June 14. West had raided the same village a year earlier, shortly after his father and brothers had been killed in the spring of 1863 by Union soldiers or citizens, and now he was back for a second visit. The Rebels came charging into town, yelling and firing their weapons, and quickly had possession of the place. Melville had been largely abandoned by the local militia, who were off on a scout in the Horse Creek vicinity, and those who remained in the village hightailed it for the woods at the first alarm, along with other male citizens. A few, however, were captured before they could make it to safety, and they were "ruthlessly shot down by the fiendish desperadoes." The victim included a sixteen-year-old lad and a blind Negro man. Said one observer, "The evident determination of the fiends was to spare the life of no one old enough to carry a gun."[41]

No women of the village were hurt, but in a few cases they were robbed of greenbacks and threatened with death if they didn't fork over. After pillaging the stores, the bushwhackers set every building in town ablaze, although the intrepid women managed to put the fires out in four or five instances. The rest of the town went up in flames, including the post office and the stores that had just been looted. Around eight a.m., the guerrillas rode out of town "gorged with plunder and sated with revenge." They headed northwest toward White Hare, the same direction from which they'd come, burning houses on the Sac River as they went. No one from Melville, however, bothered to inform the commanding officer at nearby Greenfield until two o'clock in the afternoon, forestalling a pursuit until it was too late to overtake the Rebels.[42]

A search was finally organized late in the afternoon, and the next day around noon the Federal pursuers came upon the Rebels camped in the Horse Creek vicinity, where they were busy dividing up the loot taken from Melville the day before. The Federals immediately charged, killing seven guerrillas and scattering the rest, but they were "too fatigued" to continue the chase after the fleeing Rebels. Instead, they turned their attention to gathering up goods that had been stolen the previous day and that the guerrillas had left on the ground during their hasty departure.[43]

On October 25, the same day as the Battle of Mine Creek, as Price's army was retreating down the Kansas-Missouri border, a party of Rebels estimated at 250 made a dash on Clinton but were repulsed by "seventy militia, citizen, and negroes." Five Rebels were wounded and one taken prisoner, while no Union men were reportedly hurt.[44]

By the end of 1864, conditions in Henry, St. Clair, and other counties in the second tier east of the border were even quieter than they had been in the spring. Colonel John F. Philips of the Seventh Cavalry Missouri State Militia reported in late December from the headquarters of the District of Central Missouri at Warrensburg that the "portion of the district south of the Pacific Railroad is remarkably quiet; no disturbance of any kind has occurred there for some time." Philips, therefore, relieved from duty a company at Calhoun and part of another company at Osceola, leaving only fifty men, which he deemed a sufficient number, to act in conjunction with local citizens for the protection of the area. Thus, the war in Henry and St. Clair counties, which had been winding down for more than a year, ended not with a bang but with a whimper.[45]

11
Price's Retreat and the Battle of
Mine Creek

From the time General Price and his army were forced out of Missouri early in the war, he had longed to re-enter his adopted state and try to reclaim it for the South. Finally in late August of 1864 Confederate officials approved such an effort, and Price was given command of the expedition. His Army of Missouri consisted of three divisions under Major General James F. Fagan, Brigadier General John S. Marmaduke, and Brigadier General Jo Shelby, totaling nearly 12,000 men. However, about one third of them were unarmed, as Price was forced to fill out his army with conscripts, deserters, and other irregulars.

Organization of the command was completed at Pocahontas, Arkansas, in mid-September. Price's army crossed the border into southeast Missouri on September 19 and marched north toward St. Louis. On the 27th the Confederates attacked a small Federal force under Brigadier General Thomas Ewing, Jr. at Pilot Knob and were repulsed with heavy casualties. Adding to the Confederate humiliation, Ewing slipped off during the night before Price could bring up all of his force for another attack. Although Ewing was forced to retire in the face of overwhelming Confederate numbers, the unexpected resistance Price encountered at Pilot Knob prompted him to reconsider his plan to march on St. Louis.

He veered northwest toward Jefferson City, but by the time he got there, Federal reinforcements had arrived and Price declined to make an assault on the state capital. Bypassing Jefferson City, he marched west along the Missouri River toward Kansas City with Major General Alfred Pleasonton and a large contingent of Federal troops in warm pursuit.[1]

General Sterling Price led a raid through Missouri in the fall of 1864. *Courtesy Library of Congress.*

Meanwhile, Major General Samuel R. Curtis, commanding the Department of Kansas, prepared to receive the Rebels as they neared the border. Price chose to attack Curtis before Pleasonton could catch up. On October 23 at Westport, in what some have called the Gettysburg of the West, he hurled his Missouri troops at the Kansans for four hours, but the Federal lines did not break. Although casualties were about equal on both sides, the Rebels were forced to retreat, some of them abandoning muskets and equipment on the field, as Pleasonton closed in from the rear threatening to crush Price in a pincers movement.

Shelby's division held off the Federals long enough for Price and the rest of the command to start south along the Kansas-Missouri border with the Confederate wagon train. The Federals did not immediately press their advantage, allowing the Rebels to march twenty-four miles unmolested and camp that night on the Middle Fork of the Grand River. The next day they crossed into Kansas, moved south along the Fort Scott Road, and halted for the evening near the small village of Trading Post on the Marais des Cygnes River in Linn County.

On October 24, General Curtis, by seniority of rank, assumed command of the combined Federal forces and reorganized them into the Army of the Border. After sending most of his militia home, he gave General Blunt command of the regular Kansas troops and designated them the First Division. General Pleasonton's command of Missouri and other troops composed the Second Division. Early the same morning, the pursuit after Price resumed, and it continued throughout the day. The Federals found the Rebel trail strewn with abandoned equipment, broken-down animals, and deserters from Price's army. At eight o'clock on the evening of the 24th, about fifteen miles north of Trading Post, General Pleasonton's division took the lead, with Brigadier General John B. Sanborn commanding the advance.

With orders to press on after the enemy, Sanborn marched through darkness and pouring rain and finally met and skirmished with the Confederate pickets just north of Trading Post about midnight. Here Sanborn sent Colonel J.J. Gravely ahead with the Sixth and Eighth Cavalry regiments of the Missouri State Militia to determine the exact position of the enemy. Gravely discovered that the road leading to Trading Post passed through a gap formed by high mounds over a half mile long on either side of the road, and he found Confederates blocking the gap and commanding the summits and sides of the mounds.

When the Rebels in the road opened fire, Gravely formed his troops in a skirmish line and moved toward the base of the mounds. The Confederates halted his advance with a torrent of lead that poured down from the mounds with the fury of the incessant rain, and Gravely promptly retired to report his findings to his commanding officer. Sanborn, because of the wet, dark night and his unfamiliarity with the territory, decided to postpone a general attack until shortly before daylight.

About 4:00 a.m., October 25, he ordered Colonel Gravely, reinforced by the Fourth Iowa Cavalry, to advance and drive the Confederates from their position. As Sanborn's cavalry started forward on foot, the crests of the two hills and the gap between them were just coming into view against the dim light of approaching morning, and the Union artillery shelled the mounds with a supporting cannonade. The Rebels on the Federal right gave up their stronghold with little resistance, but those on the left stood their ground. Inch by inch Sanborn's cavalry had to fight their way up the steep and slippery slope, struggling to keep their footing, before driving the stubborn Confederates from their position.

At last a cheer went up, and a volley of musketry exploded in celebration as the Federals achieved the summit of the mound and took possession of the hills and the gap between them. On the south slope of the mounds leading to the Marais des Cygnes the Confederates abandoned wagons, horses, mules, sheep, cooking equipment, and one piece of artillery in their haste to get to the river.

Still in the pre-dawn, General Pleasonton came up and took charge of the Federal maneuvers. He ordered Sanborn to advance to the Marais des Cygnes and force a crossing. When the Federals got near the ford, they found the Rebels on the opposite side of the river busily felling trees across the road to impede the pursuit.

General Sanborn dismounted a detachment of Enrolled Missouri Militia and sent them across the river about 400 yards above the ford, from which point they were to move down the river as skirmishers against the Confederates at the crossing. At the same time Colonel John E. Phelps and his Second Arkansas Cavalry (Union) advanced along the road and engaged the enemy in a heavy exchange of fire. The Rebels promptly dropped back from the ford, having managed to fell just two trees.

The Second Arkansas, supported by the Sixth and Eighth Missouri State Militia, pursued the Confederates and found them drawn up in a line of battle on the open prairie about a half mile from the crossing. General Sanborn raced back to the ford to bring up artillery and additional troops, but Colonel Phelps declined to wait for reinforcements. Charging the enemy line, he was already forcing a grudging retreat as the Federal artillery hurried into position. When the big guns opened fire, Colonel John F. Philips's First Brigade and Lieutenant-Colonel Frederick W. Benteen's Fourth Brigade of Pleasonton's division came up at a gallop and charged the Confederate left. Sanborn then brought up the rest of his Third Brigade and joined the assault, striking the Rebels' disintegrating left side. According to Sanborn, "...the enemy gave way immediately..., and fled with such precipitancy that it seemed improbable that he would form again soon."[2]

With permission from General Pleasonton, Sanborn and the tired troops of his Third Brigade fell back to eat and rest, but Philips and Benteen kept up the chase. Only about five or six hundred yards separated Philips's advance under Lieutenant-Colonel Bazel F.

Lazear from the retreating enemy as the Federals pursued the Confederates across six miles of rolling prairie that lay between the Marais des Cygnes and Mine Creek, a branch of the Little Osage.

The Confederate train stalled at the main crossing of Mine Creek, blocking the passage of the rear wagons. Because of the stream's high banks and surrounding timber, there were no other good fords in the immediate vicinity. So close was the Federal pursuit that the temporary delay threw the Rebels into confusion. General Marmaduke, commanding the rear, hastily sent word forward requesting assistance from General Fagan and informing General Price, who was several miles to the front, of the situation.

Fagan brought up eight pieces of artillery, all that were in Price's army except the three pieces that were at the head of the column with Shelby's division, and the Confederates formed a line of defense on the north side of Mine Creek. Wary of dismounting their troops in such a perilous situation, the Confederate generals decided to fight the battle on horseback, despite the fact that many of their men were armed with infantry rifles that were difficult to reload from the saddle and were, therefore, of little use in a cavalry fight. As the Rebel line formed, most of the stalled train finally managed to cross the creek, and the wagons rumbled madly across the prairie south of the stream in a desperate effort to escape.

Colonel Philips and his brigade came onto the field at a gallop and formed in a line of battle facing Marmaduke and Fagan's divisions. The Confederate artillery opened on his position, and the long Rebel line threatened to flank him on both sides. Just as the Confederate officers were about to order a charge, though, Colonel Benteen's brigade rushed up to reinforce Philips's left, and a section of Federal artillery was also hurried into position and unlimbered.

Philips, who was eager to strike the Confederate line before it could advance, immediately ordered a charge as soon as Benteen came up. As the two Federal brigades rushed forward, the Rebels unleashed an initial fire that, according to Benteen, "staggered even my own gallant regiment."[3] Regrouping, the Federals charged with such spirit that the enemy line quickly gave way. Many of the Confederates fired their infantry rifles but once, then discarded them as they wheeled their horses and fled, charging through their own rear lines and causing panic among their comrades. Seeing the mass confusion of the fleeing Confederates, the Federals screamed

135

triumphantly and renewed the charge with revolvers and sabers drawn.

In short order, the onrushing Yankees got among the terrified Rebels, slashing and shooting them down at every turn. In Benteen's words, the battle was "a fierce hand-to-hand fight, one that surpassed anything for the time it lasted I have ever witnessed."[4] According to Philips, "the fighting became general and terrific," and "the scene of death was as terrible as the victory was speedy and glorious."[5]

The Confederate commanders rode up and down the line yelling for their men to make a stand, but their exhortations failed to check the indiscriminate panic among the Rebel troops. In the words of Confederate Colonel Colton Greene, commanding Marmaduke's brigade, "The same wild panic seemed to seize everything."[6] The Federals broke through the Confederate line, and the Rebels were "completely routed and driven in the wildest confusion from the field."[7] According to Philips, "The ground in our front was strewn with the enemy's dead, dying, and wounded."[8]

As a result of the Union charge, General Marmaduke; Brigadier General William L. Cabell, General Fagan's second-in-command; several other officers; and about 400 enlisted men were cut off from their Confederate comrades and captured. In addition, the Yankees seized three Rebel flags and all eight pieces of Confederate artillery that had been brought up to the battle line.

A number of Rebel prisoners found outfitted in Federal uniforms were promptly executed for their indiscretion, while those dressed in regular Confederate gray were treated as prisoners of war. Leaving just enough of their comrades to tend to the captives, the Federals again took up the chase after the frightened and dispirited Confederate troops who fled wildly from the scene of the battle. Pressed by the Federal pursuit, many of the Rebels tossed aside their weapons and anything else that hindered their flight. According to Colonel Greene, about two-thirds of his brigade's arms were lost during the rout.

When General Price had received General Marmaduke's dispatch informing him of the enemy's advance at Mine Creek, he was riding in his carriage at the head of the Confederate train in the rear of Shelby's division, which was poised on the bank of the Little Osage. The note contained General Fagan's endorsement pledging to support Marmaduke; nevertheless, General Price immediately ordered General Shelby to take his old brigade and return to the rear to sustain Marmaduke and Fagan. Old Pap then mounted his white horse and galloped toward the rear himself to personally inspect the situation. He'd barely passed the last wagon of the Confederate train when, in his own words, he "met the divisions of Major-Generals Fagan and Marmaduke retreating in utter and indescribable confusion, many of them having thrown away their arms. They were deaf to all entreaties, and in vain were all efforts to rally them."[9]

Several officers joined General Price in trying to rally the Confederate soldiers who still had arms, but to no avail. They were racing south in an all-out flight, and neither cursing nor cajoling could harness them.

Price then ordered General Shelby to check the advancing enemy long enough to let the Confederate train cross the Little Osage and get safely away. Once again it was left to Shelby to save Price's army from utter destruction, and again the Iron Brigade rose to the task.

General Sanborn, who had stopped north of Mine Creek to let his Third Brigade rest and eat, rushed forward at the sound of guns and arrived at the creek just as the battle was over. Pushing forward, he relieved Philips's First Brigade of the advance about three miles south of Mine Creek and took up the chase after the fleeing Confederates across eight miles of prairie. About a mile north of the Little Osage, Sanborn came upon the Iron Brigade, commanded by Brigadier General Jeff Thompson, and another regiment of Shelby's division drawn up in a line. As soon as General Sanborn formed his men and started to advance, Shelby withdrew his troops to the timber along the Little Osage and there deployed his men again.

As Sanborn approached the stream, General Pleasonton sent forward a command to charge, and the Federals promptly threw themselves into the timber, driving the Confederates from the brush and across the river to a ridge about a mile beyond the Little Osage, where Shelby again halted and formed his men in three lines, determined this time to make a stand.

Here, General John McNeil's Third Brigade finally got to the Federal front after tarrying in the rear throughout the morning, and General Pleasonton now had his entire division on the field facing Shelby. Shelby's men commanded a strong position along the ridge, some of them partly protected from a Federal charge by the fences of a cornfield. The two sides skirmished for half an hour or more,

137

probing each other for a weakness, before General Pleasonton finally ordered an advance.

On the Federal left, Colonel Joseph A. Eppstein's Fifth Missouri State Militia dismounted and charged the cornfield on foot while the right moved forward on horseback at a walk. "I endeavored to charge...," General McNeil explained later, "but the utmost exertions of officers and men could not move the horses to a trot or a gallop."[10] However, the gradual Federal advance steadily drove the Confederates back, threatened to surround the cornfield, and forced the Rebels to abandon their position there. The Confederate flight resumed across four more miles of prairie, with the Rebels abandoning animals, guns, and equipment all along the way. Several times Shelby feigned a stand, only to retire as soon as Sanborn or McNeil, at the head of the Federal pursuit, made a charge.

Shelby's report describes the running fight in such glowing terms that the Rebels' humiliating retreat sounds almost like a victory. On the Federal side, General Curtis also viewed the "great panorama" with a romantic eye:

> Being mostly a prairie country the troops of both armies were in full view, and the rapid onward movement of the whole force presented the most extensive, beautiful and animated view of hostile armies I have ever witnessed. Spread over vast prairies, some moving at full speed in column, some in double lines, and others as skirmishers, groups striving in utmost efforts, and shifting as occasion required, while the great clouds of living masses moved steadily southward, presented a picture of prairie scenery such as neither man nor pencil can delineate.[11]

General Thompson, commanding Shelby's brigade, offered a more sober and realistic assessment of the action, saying simply that "Our lines were formed and broken several times this day, but our loss was small."[12]

Eight miles north of Fort Scott, Sanborn paused to let his exhausted troops rest, but General McNeil's Second Brigade kept up the pursuit and was soon joined by Colonel Benteen's Fourth. Following the path of the Rebel retreat, the Federal advance left the Fort Scott Road and moved off in a southeasterly direction. Six miles northeast of Fort Scott, McNeil and Benteen came upon Price's entire army drawn up in an impressive battle formation at a small stream called Shiloh Creek.

General Fagan and General John B. Clark, Jr., Marmaduke's second-in-command, had finally managed to rally and form their battered divisions, including those troops who had discarded their weapons during their mad flight. Along with the rest of Price's army they were drawn up in quadruple battle lines, their immense numbers outflanking the Federals by three-quarters of a mile on either side. Shelby's division, the only real fighting force that remained among the Confederates, held the front in this imposing show of strength.

Colonel Nelson Cole, Chief of Artillery, brought up ten pieces of Federal artillery and began shelling the center of the Confederate lines. General McNeil formed the Second and Fourth Brigades into a double line of battle and ordered a charge, but the jaded Federal horses could scarcely be urged into a walk. The advancing Union line met a stiff resistance from Shelby's division, and the two sides exchanged a lively fire before the Confederates finally dropped back a short distance.

Shelby now brought up reinforcements and extended his line, threatening to encircle McNeil on either side. Colonel Cole turned his guns on the extreme flanks of the Confederates, and, although his barrage landed so close to some of his own comrades that it created momentary panic in the Federal lines, he managed to drive the enemy back. Cole then once again turned his fire on the Rebel center, and the Federals soon broke the Confederate line.

The skirmish, however, bought General Price enough time for his train to reach the Marmaton River eight miles east of Fort Scott, and his army now moved off rapidly in that direction. Around midnight the last of the Southern troops crossed the Marmaton, where Price halted for about an hour to form the disheartened soldiers into some semblance of military order. Here also, finally convinced that the train he'd sacrificed so much to save was only slowing him down and threatening the annihilation of his army, he destroyed the wagons and blew up the artillery ammunition of the guns that had fallen into Federal hands. Then his ragged army moved off toward Carthage in the middle of the night, while most of the Federal troops retired to Fort Scott in search of food and rest.

Price's army had a large number of guerrillas and other irregulars who destroyed property and committed atrocities all along the path of the Southern retreat both before and after the action at

Mine Creek. On the Federal side, jayhawkers like Jennison (of Blunt's Kansas division) executed Confederate stragglers and pillaged indiscriminately as they chased the fleeing Rebels down the border.[13]

12
Newtonia and Newtonia

After the Federal victory at Pea Ridge in the spring of 1862, the Confederacy virtually abandoned Missouri, and, Federal officials, having secured the state for the Union, likewise sent most of their forces to campaigns in the East.

In the summer of 1862, though, when Confederate Major General Theophilus H. Holmes replaced General Hindman as commander of the Trans-Mississippi Department, he was eager to re-establish a Confederate presence in southwest Missouri. The region was rich in farmland and grain, and the mines at Granby produced lead that could be used in the manufacture of ammunition. Hoping to tap these resources, General Holmes ordered camps established in the area of Newtonia.

About the 9th of September, Colonel Jo Shelby's newly formed Missouri Brigade was sent to Camp Kearney (often called Camp Coffee) about six miles south of Newtonia to begin carrying out the Confederate mission. On the 13th, Shelby marched to Newtonia and attacked the Union detachment there. Although Colonel Upton Hays was killed in the skirmish, Shelby routed the Federals, driving them about ten miles toward Sarcoxie.

Moving north from Newtonia the next day, the Missouri Brigade attacked and routed some of Colonel William A. Phillips's Federal Indian troops near Carthage. After that, the Rebels skirmished twice more with Phillips at Mount Vernon thirty miles from Newtonia. Also, on September 23, five companies of Shelby's brigade rode into Granby and drove out the Federals who had been occupying the town and overseeing the working of the lead mines. The Yankees fled in confusion, leaving a supply of lead that had already been mined, and Shelby's men loaded it into wagons and hauled it back to camp.

Returning to Camp Coffee, Shelby was joined on September 27 by Colonel Douglas H. Cooper with his Confederate Indian Brigade. Cooper, by virtue of his seniority in rank over Shelby, took command of Confederate operations in southwest Missouri. He sent Colonel T.C. Hawpe of the 31st Texas Cavalry and Major J.M. Bryan of the 1st Cherokee Battalion to establish an outpost at Newtonia and to get the mill there up and running in order to supply the command with bread.

Alarmed by Shelby's September forays in southwest Missouri, Federal officials began to concentrate their forces at Sarcoxie to counter the increased Confederate activity around Newtonia. On September 29, Brigadier General Frederick Salomon sent out scouting parties from Sarcoxie, including one under Colonel Edward Lynde of the Ninth Kansas Cavalry, who marched toward Newtonia with about 150 men and two mountain howitzers. A few miles outside town, Lynde encountered the pickets of Colonel Hawpe and Major Bryan and drove them in. A mile and a quarter north of town, the Federals discovered a stronger enemy outpost near an abandoned farmhouse. Unlimbering his artillery, Lynde shelled the deserted house and nearby cornfield, and the Confederates quickly fell back and took shelter in the town. The Federals advanced to within three-quarters of a mile and again opened with their big guns, but the distance was too great to do any damage. Upon learning from captured prisoners that the Rebel strength at Newtonia was about 2,600 men, Lynde withdrew to the prairie north of Shoal Creek, made camp, and then rode back to Sarcoxie to report to General Salomon.

The general, upon hearing the cannon fire in the direction of Newtonia, had dispatched Lieutenant-Colonel Arthur Jacobi of the Ninth Wisconsin Infantry with two companies and a battery of three cannons to reinforce Colonel Lynde. When he heard Lynde's report, he sent two more companies of infantry to reinforce Jacobi, while Lynde returned to his camp north of Shoal Creek.

Lieutenant-Colonel Jacobi camped the night of September 29 about three miles from Newtonia, and the next day at daylight he moved on the Rebel position, driving in the pickets a mile north of town. He deployed his command for an assault and shelled the town with artillery from long distance. The Confederates fell back and took shelter in several brick buildings, including a large stone barn, and behind a stone wall.

Ritchey Mansion was a Confederate headquarters during the First Battle of Newtonia. *Author photo.*

Colonel Lynde, with his detachment, arrived on the scene to take command of the Federal attack and ordered the artillery, flanked by infantry on either side, to advance to a ridge overlooking the town northwest of Newtonia. Seeing that the cannonading from this point was still not effective, Lynde directed the howitzers to advance within 600 yards of the stone barn. Once in position, the big guns again opened fire on the fortified Confederates, and the infantry advanced to within a few hundred yards.

At this point a captain from Coffee's regiment arrived on the scene as a messenger of Colonel Cooper and began cursing Hawpe's Texans, calling them cowards, and ordering them to charge. Although Hawpe had never seen the man before, many of his troops obeyed the order, leaping over the stone fence to briefly check the Federal advance before being driven back to their original position. The besieged Rebels then dug in and repulsed the assault with "a perfect stream of fire right into the ranks of the infantry."[1]

As the Federals fell back, they saw Confederate reinforcements in the form of Lieutenant-Colonel Tandy Walker's First Choctaw and Chickasaw Regiment coming up on their rear and right flank, and Colonel Lynde was forced to retire with "the enemy

143

swarming from their concealed positions in the town to harass" the retreat.[2]

With Colonel Cooper, who'd arrived with the fresh troops, personally leading the charge, the Confederates raced after the fleeing Federals, seeking to press their advantage. Colonel Lynde withdrew in orderly fashion, forming and re-forming as he retreated, but at one point the Rebel charge threatened to annihilate the Ninth Wisconsin Infantry as "the fire of the enemy was terrific."[3]

The Confederates kept up the chase for three miles before Union reinforcements under Colonel William Judson, sent out by General Saloman, came up and enabled the Federals to make a stand and halt the Rebel pursuit. Seeing the additional troops, the Confederates dropped back to Newtonia at about 10:00 a.m. to await another attack.

Backed by a battery of mountain howitzers, Judson pursued the Rebels and renewed the bombardment of Newtonia from the same ridge where Federal artillery had boomed away earlier that morning. At about two in the afternoon he was reinforced by Colonel Phillips's Indian regiment and Colonel William Weer's Tenth Kansas Infantry Brigade, and the Federals once again advanced on the town. The Confederates answered the Federal cannonading with artillery they had lodged inside the stone barn. The lively exchange of artillery moved one Union soldier to describe the battle as "a beautiful sight, with just enough excitement to give it a 'delicious flavor.' …The thundering of our own guns, the spiteful reply of the enemy, the peculiarly whizzing music of the shells and shot as they fly through the air, and the crash of the destructive missiles as they plow up the ground…gives an excitement better felt than expressed."[4]

The Confederates finally repulsed the Federal assault and then launched a counter attack with the First Cherokee Battalion and the First Choctaw and Chickasaw Regiment shouting war whoops and leading the charge. At about 5:30 p.m., according to Major Bryan of the First Cherokee, "the enemy gave way the second time, and again pursued by our cavalry and a part of our artillery until darkness put an end to the pursuit."[5]

Colonel Cooper reported his loss at Newtonia as twelve killed, sixty-three wounded, and three missing for a total of seventy-eight casualties. General Saloman did not report his casualties, but Colonel Weer's report of October 1 is a good indication that Federal losses were probably significantly greater than the Confederate total. "Four whole companies of the Ninth Wisconsin," said Weer, "except about 10 men, are killed, wounded, or captured, besides others of the Sixth and Ninth Kansas and Third Indian." A Union soldier engaged in the action estimated the Federal loss at about 225 in killed, wounded, and missing, and he confirmed that the Ninth Wisconsin sustained most of the casualties.[6]

The Confederates held Newtonia for only four more days. On October 4 they retreated in the face of growing enemy strength in the area, and three columns of Union soldiers marched in and took possession of the town, once again driving the Rebels out of southwest Missouri.

A point of historical significance about the first Newtonia battle is that it was one of the few engagements of the Civil War, if not the only one, in which regimental-sized units composed of American Indians fought on opposite sides.[7]

*****

After its defeat at Westport and Mine Creek in October of 1864, Price's army was in headlong retreat down the western edge of Missouri. At the Marmaton River, Price burned and abandoned most of his wagon train and managed by hard marches to put some distance between his army and the pursuing Federals. The Rebels approached Newtonia in the early afternoon of October 28 with Brigadier General Jeff Thompson, commanding Shelby's brigade of Shelby's division, in advance. Thompson charged the garrison at Newtonia, driving out the small force stationed there. As the Yankees took flight, Thompson's advance managed to overtake and kill Captain R.H. Christian, commander at the post, who, according to Thompson, "was noted for his bloodthirsty brutality" and whom General Price dismissed as "a notorious bushwhacker."[8]

General Shelby passed Newtonia and stopped for the evening about a mile beyond the town while the other divisions of Price's army proceeded farther south and went into camp. About three p.m. General James G. Blunt, having left the rest of the Federal pursuit behind, caught up to the Confederates with two brigades of his First Division of the Army of the Border. Upon discovering Shelby's division going into camp just south of Newtonia, Blunt deployed his forces in a line on the prairie facing the Rebels. Because of intervening fences, he dismounted many of his men and ordered an advance. Supported by the heavy guns of the First Colorado Battery located on the ridge west of town, the Federals, numbering about 1,000, marched across the prairie toward the enemy to the edge of an enclosed field.

Shelby dismounted all of his men and formed a line of battle to meet the Federal attack at the opposite fence row, and firing began immediately. The Confederate line held, and the Rebels, despite heavy fire from the artillery of the First Colorado Battery, crossed the first fence and drove the Yankees back onto the prairie. The Federals remounted and dropped back to form a second skirmish line, but the Confederates crossed the second fence and continued to press Blunt's outnumbered troops.

As sundown approached, Brigadier General Sanborn arrived with the Third Brigade of Major General Pleasonton's Cavalry division and found Blunt heavily engaged, both his left and right flanks retreating in the face of the Rebel advance and threatening to give way. Blunt hastily ordered Sanborn to support his left and try to turn the enemy right flank. Sanborn dismounted his men, and, advancing on foot, they soon checked Shelby's right. Rejuvenated by the timely arrival of reinforcements, Blunt's right made a stand as well, and the Federals soon repulsed the Confederate attack. The Union cavalry made a halfhearted pursuit before returning to Newtonia for the night, as the Rebels retreated south of town.

Both sides claimed victory in the second engagement at Newtonia. Price said that after Shelby drove Blunt's forces across the prairie, "This was the last we saw of the enemy."[9] General Sanborn, on the other hand, said that the Federal cavalry drove the fleeing Confederates for three miles before calling off their pursuit on account of darkness and fatigue, and General Curtis's assistant adjutant general, Major Chapman S. Charlot, proclaimed that "our victory was complete."[10]

In terms of casualties, the battle (actually little more than a skirmish) was also a stalemate. Although General Blunt called the engagement "the warmest contested field" his Kansas troops had experienced during the campaign, the loss on each side was a mere handful killed and approximately a hundred wounded and captured.[11] However, the Rebel troops were eventually forced to retire from the field and resume their retreat South. In so doing, as one Union officer put it, they "left the historical field of Newtonia in Federal hands."[12]

According to legend, the floor of the "black room" of the Ritchey Mansion, used as a hospital during both Newtonia battles, was painted black to cover up the blood stains. *Photo by the author.*

Except for sporadic skirmishes by guerrillas, Price's retreat from Newtonia marked the end of the Confederate war effort in Missouri. The mission Old Pap had begun more than a month earlier with the high hope of taking back his home state had ended not in glory and triumph but in defeat and humiliation. His army and the Confederate States of America for which it fought were beaten, and it was now just a matter of time before formal treaties would make it official.

Although defeated, Price and many other die-hard Southerners could never submit to conquest. Near the close of the war, they traipsed off to Mexico rather than live under the umbrella of the Federal government they'd opposed so vigorously. Jo Shelby, the only Southern commander never to surrender, took his entire brigade to Mexico and, in vain, offered its service to Emperor Ferdinand Maximilian. Both Price and Shelby eventually returned to Missouri in 1867.

Many Southern-leaning Missouri citizens, like their military leaders, balked at repatriation. In certain areas of the state of Missouri, including some of the counties along the lower Kansas border, resentment toward the Federal government ran deeper even than it did in the Confederate states of the South. Citizens who at the beginning of hostilities had tried to stay neutral, who viewed the presence of the Federal army as four years of foreign occupation, and who had seen the war degenerate into savage guerrilla fighting that produced atrocities on both sides felt more justified in branding the strife that had rent their state apart as the War of Northern Aggression than the Southerners who'd dubbed it such, and many clung to their bitterness long after Reconstruction had restored the seceding states to the Union.

For their part, Kansans and loyalist Missourians harbored a resentment of their own. Throughout the war, they'd viewed Confederate sympathizers as traitors and considered bushwhackers common criminals, and, like their enemies, many of them carried their rancor to their graves. As Colonel Fitz Warren had suggested in the summer of 1862 when the Civil War was but a year old, the bitter feeling that characterized the conflict in Missouri was "an inveterate, malignant hatred" that would "last to the end of life."[13]

Appendix

Civil War Museums and Exhibits in the Lower Kansas-Missouri Border Area

Barton County Historical Society and Museum, in the basement of the courthouse, Lamar, Missouri. The museum itself has limited artifacts and information pertaining to the Civil War, but a cannon used on a Union gunboat on the Mississippi River is located on the grounds of the courthouse. Placed there in 1910 as a memorial to soldiers and sailors of the Civil War, it was rededicated in 1985 to Barton County veterans of the Civil War and subsequent American wars. The museum is open 1-4 p.m. Monday through Friday. Phone 417-682-4141. Email museum@bartoncountyhistorical.org.

Battle of Carthage Civil War Museum, 205 Grant Street, Carthage, Missouri. Dedicated to preserving the history of the Battle of Carthage, the museum is open all year 8:30 a.m-5:00 p.m. Tuesday through Saturday and 1:00 p.m.-5:00 p.m. on Sunday. Phone: 417-237-7060. The museum features a ten-minute video about the Civil War in the Ozarks, a miniature replica of the Battle of Carthage showing the deployment of forces north of town and through the streets of Carthage, and historic relics relating to the Civil War. Admission is free.

Other points of interest in the area include the Battle of Carthage State Historic Site at the east edge of town on Chestnut Street and the Kendrick Place just north of town. A tour of the mansion at the latter location, which served as Shelby's headquarters during his retreat to Arkansas after his raid into Missouri in 1863, is available by appointment (phone: 417-358-0636).

Bates County Museum, 802 Elks Drive, Butler, Missouri. This is a general-interest museum, but it contains several Civil War displays, including exhibits about General Jo Shelby, Order #11, and the Battle of Island Mound. The museum is open from April through October. Hours are from 9:30 a.m-4:00 p.m. Tuesday through Friday and 9:30 a.m.-12 noon on Saturday. Admission is $5.00 for adults,

$2.00 for students 6-17, and free for children 5 and under. Phone: 660-679-0134. Email: director@batescountymuseum.org.

Other points of interest in the area include the Battle of Island Mound State Historic Site located about eight miles southwest of Butler. Among its features are a historical plaque and a story board about the battle.

Baxter Springs Heritage Center and Museum, Eighth and East Avenues, Baxter Springs, Kansas. The museum is open Monday through Saturday from 10:00 a.m. to 4:30 p.m. and on Sunday from 1:00 p.m. to 4:00 p.m. Phone: 620-856-2385. Email: heritagectr@embarqmail.com. Admission is free. Although a general historical museum, the BSHM has several displays and considerable information relating to Quantrill's battle and massacre at Baxter Springs.

A self-guided driving tour of twelve points of interest pertaining to Quantrill's attack is available. Among the points of interest are a reconstruction of Fort Blair on the site of the original fort and a monument in the national cemetery where most of victims of the attack are buried.

Bushwhacker Museum, 212 W. Walnut Street, Nevada, Missouri. A considerable portion of this museum focuses on the Civil War and serves as a memorial to Nevada's reputation during the war as the "Bushwhacker Capital." Hours are 10:00 a.m. to 4:00 p.m., Wednesday through Saturday, from May 1 to October 1 and other times by arrangement. Admission is $5.00 for adults, $2.00 for youth 12-17, and $1.00 for children under 12. Admission to the museum includes admission to the nearby Bushwhacker Jail. Phone: 417-667-9602.

Nevada also holds an annual "Bushwhacker Days" celebration in June.

Dorothea B. Hoover Historical Museum, 7th and Schifferdecker (in Schifferdecker Park), Joplin, Missouri. Phone: 417-623-1180. Email: Joplinmuseum@sbcglobal.net. Part of the Joplin Museum Complex, this is a general historical museum, but it has at least one display containing memorabilia and information about the Civil War in the Ozarks. Hours are 10 a.m. to 7 p.m. on Tuesday and 10 a.m. to 5 p.m. Wednesday through Saturday. Admission is free on Tuesday and $2.00 per adult on other days. A monument to the soldiers who were killed during Tom Livingston's attack at the Rader farm on May 18, 1863, is located in front of the museum.

Other points of interest in the area include the Sherwood/ Rader Farm Jasper County Civil War Park about three miles north of the museum, which marks the approximate site of the Rader farm attack.

Fort Scott National Historic Site. Old Fort Boulevard, Fort Scott, Kansas. The site features a tour of the military post, restored and reconstructed as it appeared prior to and during the Civil War. Although emphasis is on the 1840s era, the visitors' center contains books and other information about the Civil War. Admission is free. Hours are 8:00 a.m. to 5:00 p.m. daily from May through October and 8:30 a.m. to 4:30 p.m. from November through April. The site is closed on Thanksgiving, Christmas, and New Year's Day. Phone: 316-223-0310.

Other points of interest in the Fort Scott area include the National Cemetery.

Henry County Museum and Cultural Arts Center, 203 W. Franklin, Clinton, Missouri. This is a general-interest museum, but it has a number of Civil War artifacts. Admission is $5.00 for adults. The museum is open 10:00 a.m.-4:00 p.m. Monday through Saturday from April through December. Phone: 660-885-8414. Email: hcmus1@centurylink.net. For $3.00, the museum also offers tours of the Dorman House, where the Rebels called during their 1862 raid on Clinton and demanded that Judge Dorman hand over the keys to his store.

Linn County Museum, 307 E. Park St. (Dunlap Park), Pleasanton, Kansas. Although a general historical museum, this site focuses considerably on the Civil War era. It features several displays about the Kansas-Missouri border conflict that led up to the war, numerous artifacts and exhibits relating to the Battle of Mine Creek, and a five-minute narrative and slide show on the battle. Admission is free, but donations are welcome (as is the case with the other museums that do not charge) Hours are 9:00 a.m. to 5:00 p.m. Tuesday and Thursday, 1-5 p.m. on Saturday, or by appointment. Phone 913-352-8739.

Mine Creek Battlefield State Historic Site, 20485 Kansas Highway 52, about one-half mile west of U. S. Highway 69, near Pleasanton, Kansas. Located in an open field between the Marais des Cygnes River and Mine Creek, where much of the fighting on

151

October 25, 1864, took place, the site features story boards that describe the events and depict the deployment of troops during the running battle that occurred that day. The visitor center also has a display room containing artifacts of the battle, and outside you may follow its course along a 2.6-mile trail through prairie and timber. The self-guided tour is available dawn to dusk, and the visitor center is open 10:00 a.m. to 5:00 p.m. Wednesday through Saturday, from May through October only. Phone: 913-352-8890. Email: minecreek@kshs.org. Admission is $5.00 for adults, $1.00 for students, and free for children five and under.

Other points of interest in the area include the Historical Park at Mound City featuring Fort Montgomery, the Jayhawker Fort/ Cabin named after James Montgomery.

Newton County Historical Museum, 121 N. Washington, Neosho, Missouri. This is a general historical museum, but it contains a number of Civil War artifacts. The museum is open 12:30-4:30 p.m. daily, except holidays. Phone: 417-451-4940.

Newtonia, Highway 86, about seven miles east of Neosho, Missouri. The Newtonia battles are commemorated by a historical marker on Highway 86 at the edge of the village and by story boards on the grounds of the Ritchey Mansion in town. This home, used as a headquarters and hospital at various times during the war by both sides, is owned and maintained by the Newtonia Battlefields Protection Association. Tours of the mansion are available by appointment. Call Tom at 417-437-5974 to arrange a tour.

Pea Ridge National Military Park, Pea Ridge, Arkansas (east of Rogers on Highway 62). The park features a driving tour of the field where the Battle of Pea Ridge was fought on March 7 and 8, 1862. The park grounds are open year-round from 6:00 a.m. till dusk, and the visitor center is open daily from 8:30 a.m. to 4:30 p.m. except Thanksgiving, Christmas, and New Year's Day. Admission to the park is $7.00 per adult or $15.00 per carload. Phone: 479-451-8122, ext. 227.

Prairie Grove Battlefield State Park, 506 E. Douglas Street, Prairie Grove, Arkansas. The park commemorates the Battle of Prairie Grove fought on December 7, 1862, and it features both a self-guided driving tour and a self-guided walking trail of the battlefield. The visitor center is open 8:00 a.m.-5:00 p.m. daily. It is closed on Thanksgiving, Christmas Eve, Christmas Day, and New Year's Day. The self-guided tours and access to the visitor center are free. Fee to tour the historic buildings on the park grounds is $5.00 for adults, $3.00 for children 6-12, or $15.00 for a family. Phone 501-846-2990.

Trading Post Museum, about six miles north of Pleasanton, Kansas, just off Highway 69 at 5710 North 4th Street. This is a general museum, but it contains some exhibits pertaining to the Civil War and the border conflict that preceded the war. Adjacent to the museum is the Trading Post Cemetery, where four victims of the Marais Des Cygnes Massacre are buried and where a monument to the victims is located. The museum's season runs from April 1 through November 1, and the hours are 10:00 a.m. to 2:00 p.m. Wednesday through Saturday. Admission is free. Phone: 913-352-6441.

About five miles northeast of Trading Post is the Marais des Cygnes Massacre State Historic Site. Commemorating the murder of five free-soil men by proslavery border ruffians in 1858, it is located at 26426 E. 1700th Rd., Pleasanton, KS. It features exterior exhibits and is open dawn to dusk for self-guided tours.

Wilson's Creek National Battlefield, 6424 West Farm Road 182, Republic, Missouri (about three miles east of Republic or ten miles southwest of Springfield). Commemorating the Battle of Wilson's Creek fought on August 10, 1861, the site features an automobile tour of the battlefield with points of interest and walking trails along the way. The visitor center features numerous exhibits about the battle, an orientation film, a fiber optics map program, a bookstore, and a research library. The visitor center is open daily, except for the library, which is open Tuesday through Saturday. Hours for the visitor center vary according to the season but generally are 8:00 a.m. to 5:00 p.m. from April through October and 9:00 a.m. to 5:00 p.m. from November through March. The visitor center is closed on Thanksgiving, Christmas, and New Year's Day, and it closes at noon on Christmas Eve. Hours for the park and tour road also vary according to the season but are generally more extended than hours for the visitor center. Entrance fee to the park is $7.00 per adult or $15.00 per carload. No fee is charged during hours when the park is open but the visitor center is not. Phone: 417-732-2662, ext. 227.

End Notes

Works frequently cited are identified by the following abbreviations:

CMS   *Columbia Missouri Statesman*

CSR   Compiled Service Records of Confederate Soldiers Who Served in Organizations from the State of Missouri, Record Group 109, microfilm copies at National Archives, Kansas City branch.

HVC   *History of Vernon County, Missouri* (1887; reprint, Clinton, MO: The Printery, 1974).

LDC   *Leavenworth Daily Conservative*

OR   *War of the Rebellion: A Compilation of Official Records of the Union and Confederate Armies* (Washington, DC: Government Printing Office, 1880-1902).

SLTWMR   *St. Louis Tri-Weekly Missouri Republican*

Chapter One
Rehearsals for War and the Battle of Carthage

1. I've drawn on various sources for my general account of events in this chapter. In addition to works specifically cited in subsequent notes, these sources include Violette's *History of Missouri*, Ingenthron's *Borderland Rebellion*, Schrantz's *Jasper County in the Civil War*, and Steele and Cottrell's *Civil War in the Ozarks*.

2. Governor Jackson's reference to the approaching war as President Lincoln's "unholy crusade" is reported in the *St. Louis Republican*, 18 April 1861.

3. General Lyon's declaration that "This means war!" is quoted in Thomas L. Snead's 1886 *The Fight for Missouri*. The author was present at the Planter's Hotel meeting as an aide-de-camp to Governor Jackson.

4. Shelby's reference to the unarmed Confederate troops at Carthage as the "line of spectators" is quoted in Livingston's *History of Jasper County*, 52.

5. Cottrell, *Civil War in the Ozarks*, 3.

6. *CMS*, 26 July 1861, quoting the *Liberty Tribune*.

7. OR, vol. 3, p. 33, report of Brigadier General William Y. Slack, 7 July 1861. (All citations of the official records refer to Series 1 unless otherwise stated.)

8. *New York Times*, 11 July 1861.

Chapter Two
Jim Lane and the Skirmish at Dry Wood Creek

1. LDC, 18 June 1861. See Castel's *Frontier State at War*, the same author's "Kansas Jayhawking Raids into Western Missouri in 1861," and Goodrich's *Black Flag* for a description of activities along the border at the start of the war.

2. Goodrich, *Black Flag*, p. 11.

3. *Ibid.*, 13.

4. *OR*, vol. 3, 455.

5. CMS, 23 August 1861, quoting the *St. Louis Democrat*.

6. *OR* (Supplement), vol. 53, 435, report of General Price 4 September 1861.

7. Supplement to the Official Records, vol. 1, 246, account of Colonel John T. Hughes, 4 September 1861.

8. *HVC*, 280. The county history is my main source for the skirmishing at Dry Wood Creek. See also the *Leavenworth Weekly Conservative*, 19 September 1861 and the official records.

9. *HVC*, 280.

10. *Leavenworth Weekly Conservative*, 19 September 1861.

11. *HVC*, 283.

12. *Ibid.*

13. *Ibid.*

14. Account of Col. Hughes, 248.

15. *Ibid.*

16. *OR*, vol. 3, 163, report of Brigadier General J. H. Lane, 3 September 1861.

17. *OR* (Supplement), vol. 53, 436.

18. Lane's report, 163.

19. *Fort Scott Democrat*, 21 September 1861.

Chapter Three
The Raid on Osceola and the Burning of Humboldt

1. Supplement to the Official Records, vol. 1, 250, report of Augustus Wattles, 25 September 1861.
2. *LDC*, 9 August 1861, 16 January 1862, and *Emporia News*, 17 August 1861. Some sources (e.g. Cutler's *History of the State of Kansas*) say that Matthews got blamed for many depredations that were actually committed by others.
3. *LDC*, 21 September 1861; Cutler, History of the State of Kansas, 669; 1860 Allen County census.
4. *LDC*, 21 September 1861; *Humboldt (Kans.) Civil War Days News*, 2003.
5. *LDC*, 21 September 1861.
6. *LDC*, 21 September 1861; *Humboldt Civil War Days News*, 2003.
7. *LDC*, 21 September 1861.
8. *LDC*, 14 September 1861 and 21 September 1861.
9. *OR*, vol. 3, 490.
10. *Emporia News*, 28 September 1861; *LDC*, 26 September 1861; *Humboldt Civil War Days News*, 2003.
11. *OR*, vol. 3, 490.
12. *Ibid.*, 493. The official records say Lane cleared out "Parkville," but this was probably a reference to Parkersville, a community that existed prior to the war in northwest Bates County. According to the *History of Cass and Bates County* (p. 805), "The town was destroyed during the war of 1861. A cornfield now marks the spot where it stood."
13. *OR*, vol. 3, 196.
14. *LDC*, 26 September 1861.
15. *Ibid.*
16. *Ibid.*
17. *Ibid.* There appears to be no mention of this skirmish in the official records; so the fact and size of the skirmish are questionable.
18. The *History of St. Clair County* says Lane arrived on the evening of the 23rd and left on the 24th, but this is an error. The official records (vol. 3, p. 3) give the date of the destruction of Osceola as September 22, and other sources (see Goodrich's Black Flag, p. 18, and *LDC*, 26 September 1861 and 28 September 1861) seem to agree. Also, Lane's report of the incident, written after his retreat to the Kansas border approximately fifty miles away, is dated the 24th.

So, it's almost certain the incident occurred at least one day earlier than the county history says.

19. My account of the Osceola raid is drawn from the official records, the *History of Henry and St. Clair Counties*, the *HVC*, and contemporaneous newspaper reports of the *LDC*.

20. *HVC*, 290. All reports generally agree that no civilians were deliberately murdered during the Osceola raid. In January 1899 John Speer, who lived through the Lawrence Massacre, gave a speech to the Kansas State Historical Society recounting an October 1898 visit to Osceola during which he interviewed surviving witnesses of the 1861 raid. None claimed that civilians were wantonly murdered as they were at Lawrence.

21. HVC, 290.

22. *History of Henry and St. Clair Counties*, p. 988.

23. *Ibid*.

25. *LDC*, 28 September 1861.

26. My account of the second Humboldt raid is drawn largely from Cutler, *History of the State of Kansas*, 669. See also *LDC*, 26 October 1861.

27. *HVC*, 290-291.

Chapter Four
The War in Bates County and the Skirmish at Island Mound

1. *LDC*, 5 November 1861, quoting the *Osawatomie Herald*; Cutler, *History of the State of Kansas*, 1106. At the very outset of the Civil War, Clem organized a home guard force in Bates County to protect the border from a possible invasion from Kansas, and shortly afterward he joined the Missouri State Guard and was elected captain of a company. At the time of his raid into Kansas, he'd returned home, absent without leave from the State Guard. (See soldier's military service file, microfilm copy M322, #180, at National Archives, Kansas City branch.)

2. Ibid.

3. *LDC,* 5 November 1861, quoting the *Osawatomie Herald*; *Leavenworth Daily Times*, 17 November 1861.

4. *LDC*, 16 November 1861.

5. Norton, 35-36; *Leavenworth Daily Times*, 24 November and 7 December 1861.

6. *LDC*, 21 December 1861; Cutler, 1106-1107.

7. *Ibid.*

8. *LDC*, 20 December 1861; *History of Cass and Bates Counties, Missouri*, 858; Norton, 37.

9. *LDC*, 3 January 1862.

10. *LDC*, 7 January 1862.

11. *Ibid.*

12. Special Order #16, Headquarters Eighth Division Missouri State Guard, Brigadier General James S. Rains, dated 31 January 1862, copy in author's possession, courtesy of Susan Hejka; *OR*, vol. 8, 637; *History of Cass and Bates Counties*, 998.

13. *History of Cass and Bates Counties*, 997-1000; email correspondence with Chris Tabor, 3 July 2002; 1860 Bates County census. Three days before the Federal foraging at Elswick's farm, Elswick signed an affidavit accusing Thomas Carter of stealing from him, but it's not clear whether the two events are related. (See Union Provost Marshals Papers on Individual Citizens, microfilm copy at Missouri State Archives, Reel #F 1235.)

14. *LDC*, 7 August 1862. These might have been some of Jackman's men as reported, but in early August, Jackman himself was over a hundred miles to the south in the Arkansas-Missouri border area, from where he started north to the Battle of Lone Jack.

15. Gail Buckley, *American Patriots: The Story of Blacks in the Military from the Revolution to Desert Storm* (NY: Random House, 2001), 82-83; Joseph T. Glutthaar, *Forged in Battle: The Civil War Alliance of Black Soldiers and White Officers* (New York: The Free Press, 1990), 7 and 122.

16. *OR* (Supplement), vol. 53, 455-456; *LDC*, 9 November 1862.

17. *Ibid*; *LDC*, 4 November 1862; email correspondence with Chris Tabor, 3 July 2002.

18. *OR* (Supplement), vol. 53, 455-456.

19. *Ibid.*, 456.

20. *Ibid.*, 456-457.

21. *LDC*, 7 November 1862.

22. *OR* (Supplement), vol. 53, 457.

23. *Ibid.*

24. *LDC*, 4 November 1862, 7 November 1862, and 13 November 1862.

25. *LDC*, 29 August 1863.

26. *LDC*, 9 May 1863.

27. *OR*, vol. 22, pt. 1, 333-334.

28. *Ibid.*, 376. At least one report (*St. Louis Daily Union*, 27 June 1863) suggested that the bushwhackers who burned Butler were part of Jasper County guerrilla Tom Livingston's command.

29. *LDC*, 29 August 1863.

30. *OR*, vol. 34, pt. 2, 537, 803, and pt. 3, 156.

Chapter Five
John T. Coffee and the Non-Confederate Rebellion

1. John K. Hulston and James W. Goodrich, "John Trousdale Coffee," *Missouri Historical Review* 77, no. 3 (April 1983): 273-276.

2. *Ibid.*, 276-278. See also the 1883 *History of Greene County, Missouri*, 241-242.

3. *St. Louis Daily Missouri Democrat*, 11 July 1861; *SLTWMR*, 1 August 1861.

4. CSR, M322, #180, Coffee's military service file.

5. *OR*, vol. 8, 75, report of Colonel Clark Wright, 27 February 1862.

6. Norton, *Behind Enemy Lines*, 50-52.

7. *OR*, vol. 13, 94.

8. Supplement to the Official Records, vol. 3, 30.

9. *OR*, vol. 13, 409; *SLTWMR*, 13 June 1862; *St. Joseph Weekly Herald*, 19 June 1862, quoting the *Springfield Missourian*.

10. *OR*, vol. 13, 409.

11. *Ibid.*, 858.

12. *OR*, vol. 13, 472; Norton, 64-66.

13, *OR*, vol. 13, 528, 542, 545, and 555.

14. *Ibid.*, 530.

15. Britton, *Civil War on the Border*, vol. 2, 106-108.

16. *Ibid.*

17. *OR*, vol. 13, 531.

18. *Ibid.*, 537.

19. *HVC*, 305.

20. *HVC*, 305; OR, vol. 13, 210-211.

21. *HVC*, 305

22. *Ibid.*, 306.

23. *Ibid*

24. *OR*, vol. 13, 543; *LDC*, 22 August 1862.

25. *HVC*, 306; *LDC*, 19 August 1862.

26. *LDC*, 19 August 1862.

27. *OR*, vol. 13, 221.

28. *OR*, vol. 13, 221; *HVC*, 308-309.

29. *Fort Scott Bulletin*, 9 August 1862.

30. *OR*, vol. 13, 549.

31. *Ibid.*, 230.

32. *LDC*, 22 August 1862.

33. *OR*, vol. 13, 230, 566, and 571; Norton, 84-89.

34. *OR*, vol. 13, 252; *Leavenworth Daily Times*, 29 August 1862.

35. *OR*, vol. 13, 615; Norton, 121.

36. Peter Wellington Alexander papers, letter dated 1 September 1862 from Colonel Emmett MacDonald to General Hindman; Norton, 128.

37. *LDC*, 30 September 1862.

38. *OR*, vol. 13, 979.

39. OR, vol. 13, 48, vol. 22, pt. 1, 903-904; Carolyn M. Bartels, transcriber, *Confederate States Army Trans-Mississippi Order and Letter Book*, (Two Trails Publishing, 2000), 13 and 25.

40. Peter Wellington Alexander papers, letter dated 5 November 1862 from John S. Marmaduke to Thomas C. Hindman.

41. *OR*, vol. 22, pt. 1, 321-322; pt. 2, 7 and 145; Norton, 131.

42. *OR*, vol. 22, pt. 1, 337.

43. *OR*, vol. 22, pt. 1, p. 338; Livingston, *History of Jasper County*, 62.

44. *OR*, vol. 22, pt. 2, p. 849

45. *Ibid.* 393.

46. *Ibid.*, 412.

47. *Ibid.*

48. *Ibid.*, 438.

49. *OR*, vol. 22, pt. 1, 553-554; *SLTWMR*, 17 August 1863.

50. *OR*, vol. 22, pt. 1, 613; vol. 4 (Supplement), 156; *Macon Gazette*, 24 September 1863.

51. OR, vol. 22, pt. 1, 656; *Howard County Advertiser*, 25 December 1863.

52. Hulston and Goodrich, 288; *SLTWMR*, 30 October 1863.

53. Hulston and Goodrich, 288.

54. *SLTWMR*, 21 October 1863, quoting the *Boonville Central Advertiser*, 17 October 1863.

55. *Confederate States Army Trans-Mississippi Order and Letter Book*, 27.

56. OR, vol. 41, pt. 1, 642; pt. 3, 978; Norton, 193.

57. Hulston and Goodrich, 293-294; CSR, M322, #180; Norton, 132. See also OR, vol. 48, pt. 2, 586 and *Confederate Organizations, Officers, and Posts 1861-1865: Missouri Units*, 46.

Chapter Six
Tom Livingston and the Burning of Sherwood

1. Ward L. Schrantz, *Jasper County in the Civil War* (1923; reprint, Carthage, Mo.: Kiwanis Club, 1988), 104; 1860 Jasper County census. Schrantz called Livingston a bachelor, perhaps because he was living with William Parkinson and Parkinson's wife, Sarah, with no children in the household at the time of the 1860 census. However, Livingston was, in fact, a widower. His two children had been sent to live with relatives after their mother's death.
2. Petersen et al. *Sterling Price's Lieutenants*, 276; *LDC*, 21 September 1861; *Humboldt Civil War Days News*, 2003. Although Livingston was associated with Talbott during the early stages of the war, some evidence suggests that he might have commanded an "independent company" that was only loosely affiliated with Talbott's Eleventh Cavalry. See, for example, the *SLTWMR*, 23 December 1861. Also, Britton (*The Civil War on the Border*, 1898) characterized Livingston's command in the summer of 1861 as a guerrilla band.
3. William G. Cutler, *History of the State of Kansas*, vol. 1 (Chicago: A.T. Andreas, 1883), 669; *OR*, Series 2, vol. 1, 135; *LDC*, 26 October 1861.
4. Cutler, *History of the State of Kansas*, 669; *OR*, Series 2, vol. 1, 135.
5. Joel T. Livingston, *History of Jasper County*, vol. 1 (Chicago: The Lewis Publishing Company, 1912), 54.
6. *Ibid*.
7. Petersen, et. al., 276; *Confederate Organizations, Officers, and Posts 1861-1865: Missouri Units* (Springfield, Mo.: Ozarks Genealogical Society, Inc., 1988), 1. See also *OR*, vol. 22, pt. 1, 321-322, for evidence of Livingston's Confederate authority. Two articles in the *Carthage Evening Press* (11 July 1938 and 11 July 1953) suggest that Livingston received a commission under the Partisan Ranger Act in the spring of 1862.
8. Schrantz, 105.

9. Marvin Van Gilder, *Jasper County: The First Two Hundred Years* (The Jasper County Commission, 1995), 88. See also *Carthage Weekly Press*, 19 October 1911.

10. *OR*, vol. 8, 749.

11. *History of Newton, Lawrence, Barry, and McDonald Counties*, pt. 1 (Chicago: Goodspeed Publishing Co., 1888) 477.

12. *Carthage Evening Press*, July 11, 1938.

13. *Fort Scott Western Volunteer*, 3 May 1862.

14. *OR*, vol. 8, 94-95.

15. *OR*, vol. 13, 858; Peter Wellington Alexander papers (microfilm copy), University of Arkansas Library, Fayetteville, letter from Colonel Emmett MacDonald to General Hindman, 11 October 1862.

16. *OR*, vol. 13, 552.

17. Livingston's *History of Jasper County* says this incident occurred in mid-June of 1862, but Shelby's report of 27 October 1862 (*OR*, vol. 13, p. 979) says that he camped on Coon Creek in August and skirmished there with Cloud. See also the *Leavenworth Daily Times*, 31 August 1861.

18. *OR*, vol. 13, 277-278 and 661.

19. *OR*, vol. 13, 277; *St. Joseph Weekly Herald*, 25 September 1862.

20. Livingston, *History of Jasper County*, 57.

21. *OR*, vol. 13, 672.

22. *Ibid.*, 744.

23. *OR*, Series 2, vol. 4, 667.

24. *OR*, vol. 13, 353; *LDC*, 16 November 1862 and 20 November 1862.

25. *OR*, vol. 13, 353.

26. *OR*, vol. 13, 353; *Carthage Evening Press*, 11 July 1938.

27. Schrantz, 104.

28. *OR*, vol. 22, pt. 1, 874.

29. *OR*, vol. 22, pt. 2, 33.

30. *OR*, vol. 22, pt. 1, 219.

31. *OR*, vol. 22, pt. 2, 48.

32. *Ibid.*, 109.

33. *LDC*, 6 March 1863

34. *OR*, vol. 22, pt. 1, 233.

35. "Returns from Military Posts, Fort Scott, Kansas, 1859-1866" (Microfilm M617, #1137, National Archives and Records Administration, Central Plains Region, Kansas City); *OR*, vol. 22, pt. 1, 233. The returns from Fort Scott also show a skirmish between

Livingston and a detachment from the fort on January 11 below Carthage during which the guerrillas had several men taken prisoner but also took several of their own. Livingston himself was not in the Carthage area at this time, but some of his men might well have skirmished with the Fort Scott troops.

36. *OR*, vol. 22, pt. 1, 233-234.

37. *Ibid.*, 234.

38. *Ibid.*, 236.

39. *Ibid.*, 238.

40. *Ibid.*

41. *OR*, vol. 22, pt. 1, 238; Livingston, *History of Jasper County*, 59.

42. CSR, M322, #193, Livingston's military file.

43. *LDC*, 25 November 1862; F. A. North, *History of Jasper County, Missouri*, pt. 2 (Des Moines: Mills and Co., 1883), 393; *Carthage Evening Press*, 11 July 1938.

44. CSR, M322, #193.

45. *Ibid.* Following is the list of soldiers Livingston claimed to have paroled without an exchange: "Thos. Houghton, Gilbert Schooling, Silvenius Keller, Isaac N. Spencer, M.C. Wilbanks, John W. Henry, Casell Humbard belonging to Major Allen's company at Bower's Mill. Sergeant T. H. Raymore, Wm. Kinross, Thos. Cauthen, B.F. Fugate, Eli Cates, C.J. Drummond, F.M. Southard, Samuel Jones, Wm. T. Hart belonging to Major Eno's command at Newtonia. W.H. Alberty, Hugh Watkins, Oliver Hunt, Coleman Simmons, Allen Hurt, Robert E. Nealy (of) Major Eno's command. John Cook (of) Col. Phillips' command at Greenfield. Samuel Hicks (of) Capt. Henning (at) Neosho. Samuel Pearcy, Major Eno's command. Samuel Hill (of) Major Allen, Bower's Mill."

46. *OR*, vol. 22, pt. 2, 193.

47. *OR* (Supplement), vol. 53, p. 457.

48. *OR*, vol. 22, pt. 1, 320; *LDC*, 16 May 1863.

49. *OR*, Series 2, vol. 5, 503; *OR*, 22, pt. 1, 338; *LDC*, 2 June 1863; *Kansas City Weekly Western Journal of Commerce*, 30 May 1863.

50. *OR.*, vol. 22, pt. 1, 321.

51. *OR*, vol. 22, pt. 2, 282; *St. Joseph Weekly Herald*, 28 May 1863.

52. *OR*, Series 2, vol. 5, 503; *LDC*, 14 May 1863; *OR*, vol. 22, pt. 1, 330.

53. *OR*, vol. 22, pt. 1, 330.

54. *Ibid.*

55. *Ibid.*

56. *Ibid.*, 330-331.

57. *Ibid.*, 331.

58. *Ibid.*, 329.

59. *Ibid.*, 321.

60. *LDC*, 23 May 1862, 31 May 1863; *OR,* vol. 22, pt. 1, 322. See also Hugh L. Thompson, "Baxter Springs as a Military Post, 1862-1863," written in 1895 and reprinted in the *Baxter Springs News*, 1 October 1931 and Dolph Shaner, "Sherwood—The Ghost Town" in the *Joplin Globe*, 11 February 1934.

61. *OR*, vol. 22, pt. 1, 322.

62. *OR*, vol. 22, pt. 1, 322; *LDC* 23 May 1863.

63. *OR*, vol. 22, pt. 1, 322.

64. *Ibid.*

65. The Union officer's letter is quoted in William N. Pearson, *Sherwood: The Forgotten Village* (the author, 1978), 9-10.

66. Regimental Letter Book, 1st Kansas Colored Infantry (Microfilm M858, roll 5, frame 4176), National Archives and Records Administration--Central Plains Region, Kansas City.

67. *Ibid.*, frames 4177-4178.

68. *Ibid.*, frame 4179.

69. *Ibid.*, frames 4181-4182.

70. *Ibid.*, frame 4182.

71. *Ibid.* See also Thompson in *Baxter Springs News*, 1 October 1931; *OR*, vol. 22, pt. 1, 322; and Dudley T. Cornish, *The Sable Arm: Black Troops in the Union Army 1861-1865* (1956; reprint, Lawrence: University Press of Kansas, 1987), 145-146.

72. *OR*, vol. 22, pt. 1, 342.

73. Thompson in *Baxter Springs News*, October 1, 1931; *OR*, vol. 22, pt. 1, 322; *LDC*, 23 June 1863.

74. *OR*, vol. 22, pt. 2, 330.

75. *St. Louis Daily Union*, 27 June 1863.

76. *OR*, vol. 22, pt. 1, p. 445; *History of Hickory, Polk, Cedar, Dade, and Barton Counties, Missouri* (Chicago: Goodspeed Publishing Co., 1889), 423.

77. *Carthage (Weekly) Press*, October 19, 1911.

78. *Ibid.*

79. *OR*, vol. 22, pt. 1, 445; *Carthage Evening Press*, 11 July 1938; *KCDJC*, 18 July 1863.

80. *OR*, vol. 22, pt. 2, 393; Van Gilder, 89.

81. Interview with Steve Weldon, Jasper County Archivist, 29 June 1999.

Chapter Seven
The War in Vernon County and the Burning of Nevada

1. *HVC*, 269.
2. *Ibid.*, 270.
3. Connelly papers, Box 13, Kansas State Historical Society. See also *Emporia News*, 7 December 1861, 12 April 1862, 17 May 1862, 12 July 1862 and the *Kansas Cosmos*, 7 May 1886.
4. *HVC*, 296-299 for the story of Gatewood and the Riggs house fight.
5. *OR*, vol. 13, 64.
6. *OR*, vol. 13, 53-57 and *HVC*, 299-305, for the fight at the Montevallo hotel.
7. Colonel Moss's report of the hotel fight lists two killed and four wounded. The county history, however, cites the names of six men who were wounded as well as those of the two men who were killed.
8. *OR*, vol. 13, 56.
9. *Ibid.*, 57.
10. *HVC*, 310-311.
11. *Ibid.*, 311.
12. In addition to the Vernon County history, see also the *Kansas City Daily Western Journal of Commerce*, 19 May 1863, 24 May 1863, and the *LDC*, 19 May 1863, for information concerning Frizzell's murder of Baker.
13. *HVC*, 316. The county history is my main source for both the guerrilla attack at Nevada and the militia's burning of the town in retaliation.
14. *Ibid.*, 318.
15. *Ibid.*, 319.
16. *OR*, vol. 22, pt. 1, 442-443.
17. *HVC*, 321.

Chapter Eight
Quantrill and the Massacre at Baxter Springs

1. In addition to the numerous first-hand accounts cited in this chapter, I've consulted in particular Leslie's *The Devil Knows How to*

Ride and Connelley's *Quantrill and the Border Wars* for an overview of the action at Baxter Springs.

2. *OR*, vol. 13, 348 and 352.

3. *CMS,* 8 May 1863; *Kansas City Weekly Western Journal of Commerce*, 28 November 1863; 1860 Cedar County census. Some scholars have suggested that Quantrill's trip to Richmond was merely a figment of the imagination of early Quantrill apologists like John N. Edwards, but such a trip did occur. It is known from Quantrill's compiled service records (microfilm M322, #193), for instance, that he drew pay from a Confederate paymaster in Alabama in early March 1863, presumably on his return trip from Richmond. Also, at least one newspaper report in the spring of 1863 (*LDC*, 19 May 1863) suggested that Quantrill had recently returned from a trip to Richmond seeking authority to raise a regiment.

4. *Ibid.*

5. *CMS*, 8 May 1863.

6. *CMS*, 8 May 1863; Barton, *Three Years with Quantrill*, 98; *SLTWMR*, 30 April 1863, quoting the *St. Louis Union*.

7. *CMS*, 8 May 1863; *Kansas City Weekly Western Journal of Commerce*, 28 November 1863; Barton, *Three Years with Quantrill*, 98.

8. *Ibid.* and 1860 Cedar County census.

9. *CMS*, 8 May 1863.

10. Britton, *The Union Indian Brigade in the Civil War*, 313; *Fort Scott Monitor*, 8 October 1863.

11. W.H. Warner, "The Battle and Massacre at Baxter Springs, October 6, 1863," in Cutler's *History of the State of Kansas*, 1152-1153.

12. William Gregg, a Quantrill captain who wrote and was interviewed extensively about his war experiences, mentioned only himself and Pool in connection with leading the attack on the fort at Baxter Springs, and many writers have accepted his version. However, Quantrill made no mention of Gregg in his 13 October 1863 report. Instead he said that Brinker and Pool led the advance.

It's unclear exactly when Holt's company left the guerrilla command, but perhaps the recruits had continued south toward Arkansas the previous day. If so, this would account for Quantrill's estimate of his strength at 300 men.

13. In addition to the official records, see accounts of W.H. Warner in Cutler's *History of the State of Kansas*, J.J. Jones in 6 March 1884

National Tribune, and McCorkle in *Three Years with Quantrill* (135-136) for a description of Quantrill's initial attack on the fort at Baxter Springs. Jones said three of the soldiers captured by Quantrill's advance were later released. In light of the day's other events, this seems incredible, but it's corroborated by other sources (e.g. Hugh Thompson, "Baxter Springs as a Military Post, 1862-1863"). Both Jones and Thompson name one specific individual who was released—Patrick McNary.

14. *OR*, vol. 22, pt. 1, 698, report of Lieutenant James B. Pond, 7 October 1863.

15. *Ibid.*, 699.

16. *Ibid.*, 689. See also Blunt's 7 October 1863 letter to Captain Tholen at Leavenworth describing the Baxter Springs massacre. The letter was later published in newspapers, and the handwritten original is now in the Civil War Narratives box at the Kansas State Historical Society. The account in the letter essentially agrees with Blunt's official report filed twelve days later.

17 *OR*, vol. 22, pt. 1, 701, report of Colonel W.C. Quantrill, 13 October 1863.

18. *Ibid.*

19. At Baxter, the guerrillas did take at least one prisoner, a black man named Rube, who was a barber and servant for General Blunt. They took him to Texas to tend to the tonsorial needs of the bushwhackers the following winter. (They also captured a second black man but killed him the next day.) See William E. Connelley, *Quantrill and the Border Wars*, 432-433; his interview with John Koger in the Connelley Collection at the Denver Public Library, Folder 87; and Barton, (i.e. McCorkle), 138-139.

20. Blunt's letter of 7 October 1863,

21. The account of Mrs. Thomas's escape, including the quoted conversation, is from "Lydia Stevens Thomas" in *The Club Member*, vol. 4, No. 2, 1907. The facts of this account come from Charles Davis, the driver of the buggy, and it is largely confirmed by B.I. Dugdale's unpublished account of the Baxter Springs massacre at the Kansas State Historical Society. A conflicting report claims Mrs. Thomas was riding in an ambulance, that General Blunt and Major Curtis lifted her onto a horse from Blunt's personal remuda, and that she escaped while clinging to the saddle as the powerful steed leaped across the ravine. Davis's account is more credible as Blunt made no mention whatsoever of Mrs. Thomas in either his official report or

his letter written the day after the attack. A variation on the alternate version of the incident claims that it was the scout, William Tough, who lifted Mrs. Thomas onto a horse. (See *Fort Scott Union Monitor*, 15 October 1863.) It is quite possible that Tough did help lift her onto a horse, but, at least according to Davis, the buggy was already out of immediate danger at the time.

22. W.H. Warner, the post surgeon at Baxter Springs, said that some of the soldiers had members of their families at the fort at the time of Quantrill's attack and that a woman and a small child were wounded during the fight (see *Girard, [Kans.] Press*, 26 May 1870, and Cutler's *History of the State of Kansas*, 1153). J.J. Jones's letter to the *National Tribune* corroborates this statement, and Warner gave convincing specifics, such as the nature of the wounds. However, the shooting of the woman and the child was almost surely inadvertent.

23. See Fellman's *Inside War* for a perceptive analysis of the psychology of the guerrilla warfare in Missouri.

24. Dugdale's unpublished account.

25. Sgt. Jack Splane's "Tell old God..." quote was cited by Major Henning in his 7 October 1863 report, *OR*, vol. 22, pt. 1, 697.

26. Pvt. Jesse Smith's statement was also recounted by Henning.

27. Arnold's story is recounted in various sources, but see especially an October 1886 newspaper clipping at the Baxter Springs Historical Museum.

28. Quantrill's battlefield boast was recalled by Gregg in his unpublished interview with William Connelley in the Connelley papers at the Kansas State Historical Society.

29. Crawford's statement is quoted in Connelley's *Quantrill and the Border Wars*, 430.

30. *OR*, v. 22, pt. 1, 701.

31. *Ibid.* 691.

32. Britton, *The Civil War on the Border*, vol. 2, 354-359 and *OR*, vol. 34, pt. 1, 941-942, for Quantrill's attack at Lamar in the spring of 1864.

33. *CMS*, 10 June 1864.

34. Allen Palmer in the 15 September 1918 *Kansas City Star*, as quoted by Donald Hale in *We Rode With Quantrill*.

Chapter Nine
Jo Shelby and the Raid into Missouri During 1863

1. O'Flaherty, *General Jo Shelby: Undefeated Rebel*, 59. This source and Britton's *The Civil War on the Border*, in addition to the official records, are the main sources for the general account of events in this chapter.
2. *OR*, vol. 22, pt. 1, 671.
3. *Ibid.*, 671-672.
4. *Ibid.*, 672.
5. *OR*, vol. 22, pt. 1, 656.
6. *Ibid.*, 672.
7. *Ibid.*
8. *Ibid.*
9. *Ibid.*
10. *Ibid.*, 659.
11. *Ibid.*, 672.
12. *OR*, vol. 22, pt. 2, 620.
13. *OR*, vol. 22, pt. 1, 672.
14. *Ibid.*, 676.
15. *Ibid.*, 625.
16. *Ibid.*, 663.
17. *Ibid.*, 678.
18. *Ibid.*

Chapter Ten
The Second Tier of Counties and the Affair at Germantown

1. *Leavenworth Weekly Conservative*, 18 July 1861.
2. *Ibid.*, 18 July 1861 and 25 July 1861.
3. *OR,* vol. 8, 381-382.
4. *Ibid.*, 582.
5. *Ibid.*, 341-342, 604.
6. *Ibid.*, 341-343, 358, 637.
7. *OR*, vol. 13, 51-52; CSR, M322, #182. Feaster enlisted in the Confederate Army a couple of months after the skirmish at Shiloh, and he was elected captain of a company in August of 1862.
8. *OR*, vol. 13, 52-53.
9. *Ibid.*, 60-61.
10. *Ibid.*

11. *Ibid.*, 120.

12. *SLTWMR*, 2 August 1862.

13. *OR*, vol. 13, 200-201.

14. *Ibid.*, 201.

15. *Ibid.*

16. *Ibid.*

17. *SLTWMR*, 27 September 1862.

18. *Ibid.*

19. *Ibid.*

20. *SLTWMR*, 2 December 1862.

21. *Ibid.*

22. *Ibid.*

23. *Ibid.* One of the men captured in November of 1862 on Horse Creek in Cedar County, Jacob Rector, was captured again the following summer in Lawrence County and, after being imprisoned in Springfield, St. Louis, and Illinois, eventually took the oath of allegiance and joined the Federal Army. See CSR, M322, #71.

24. *SLTWMR*, 21 January 1863; Connelley, *Border Wars*, 281.

25. *SLTWMR*, 21 January 1863.

26. *Ibid.*, 9 May 1863.

27. *St. Louis Daily Union*, 18 August 1863; *OR*, vol. 13, 125; *OR*, vol. 34, pt. 2, 291; *St. Louis Daily Missouri Democrat*, 31 August 1863.

28. *St. Louis Daily Missouri Democrat*, 31 August 1863 for the execution of Dunn and Marshall; *OR*, vol. 22, pt. 1, 609-610, for the killing of Raftre. The man identified in Union correspondence as John Raftre/Rafter was probably the thirty-year-old John Raftery listed in 1860 Henry County census.

29. *St. Louis Daily Union*, 15 September 1863.

30. *OR*, vol. 22, pt. 1, 706.

31. *OR.*, vol. 34, pt. 1, 856.

32. *Ibid.* Archibald Colson, the citizen who shot the marauding Rebel in Deepwater Township in March of 1864, was a former third lieutenant in the same Missouri State Guard company in which Jerome McAbee, the Rebel killed by Captain Joe Parks in the Horse Creek vicinity in November of 1862, served as a first lieutenant. See *Confederate Organizations, Officers, and Posts 1861-1865: Missouri Units*, 32.

33. *OR*, vol. 34, pt. 1, 856.

34. *Ibid.*, 857.

35. *Ibid.*

36. *Ibid.*

37. *Ibid.*

38. *OR*, vol. 34, pt. 1, 857; *St. Louis Daily Union*, 8 April 1864.

39. *OR*, vol. 34, pt. 3, 249.

40. *OR*, vol. 34, pt. 1, 1001.

41. *OR*, vol. 34, pt. 1, 1006-1007; *SLTWMR*, 22 June 1864; A.J. Young, ed., *History of Dade County and Its People*, The Pioneer Historical Company, 1917, 116 and 237.

42. *OR*, vol. 34, pt. 1, 1006-1007; *SLTWMR*, 22 June 1864.

43. *OR*, vol. 34, pt. 1, 1009-1010.

44. *St. Louis Daily Union*, 28 October 1864.

45. *OR*, vol. 41, pt. 4, 907.

Chapter Eleven
Price's Retreat and the Battle of Mine Creek

1. *OR*, vol. 41, pt. 1, 310-312, report of General William S. Rosecrans, 7 December 1864. In addition to the official records, the main sources for the general account of events in this chapter are Castel's *General Sterling Price and the Civil War in the West*, Shalhope's *Sterling Price: Portrait of a Southerner*, and Britton's *Civil War on the Border*.

2. *OR*, vol. 41, pt. 1, 391, report of General John B. Sanborn, 13 November 1864.

3. *OR*, vol. 41, pt. 1, 332, report of Lieutenant Colonel Frederick W. Benteen, 3 November 1864.

4. *Ibid.*

5. *OR*, vol. 41, pt. 1, 352, report of Colonel John F. Philips, 7 November 1864.

6. *OR*, vol. 41, pt. 1, 691, report of Colonel Colton Greene, 18 December 1864.

7. Benteen's report of 3 November 1864, 332.

8. Philips's report of 7 November 1864, 352.

9. *OR*, vol. 41, pt. 1, 637, report of Major General Sterling Price, 28 December 1864.

10. *OR*, vol. 41, pt. 1, 373, report of Brigadier General John McNeil, 23 November 1864.

11. *OR*, vol. 41, pt. 1, 497, report of Major General Samuel R. Curtis, January 1865.

12. *OR*, vol. 41, pt. 1, 668, report of Brigadier General M. Jeff Thompson, 24 November 1864.

13. Castel, *Frontier State at War*, 196 and 228-229.

Chapter Ten
Newtonia and Newtonia

1. *OR*, vol. 13, 292, report of Colonel Edward Lynde, 1 October 1862. In addition to the official records, other sources consulted for this chapter include Castel's *General Sterling Price and the Civil War in the West*; Shalhope's *Sterling Price: Portrait of a Southerner*; Britton's *Civil War on the Border*; Robert J. Fryman, *"Engaged the Enemy Again": An Assessment of the 1862 and 1864 Civil War Battlefields at Newtonia*, Missouri (Atlanta: Garrow and Associates, Inc., 1995); and Edwin C. Bearss, "The Army of the Frontier's First Campaign: The Confederates Win at Newtonia," *Missouri Historical Review* 60, no. 3 (April 1966).

2. *OR*, vol. 13, 293.

3. *Ibid.*

4. *Leavenworth Daily Times*, 24 October 1862.

5. *OR*, vol. 13, 301, report of Major J. M. Bryan, 12 October 1862.

6. *OR*, vol. 13, 288; *Leavenworth Daily Times*, 17 October 1862.

7. Interview with Newton County historian Kay Hively, 10 July 1999.

8. *OR,* vol. 41, pt. 1, 638 and 669.

9. *Ibid.*, 638.

10. *Ibid.*, 392 and 528.

11. *LDC*, 3 November 1864 and 5 November 1864.

12. *OR*, vol. 41, pt. 1, 405, report of Colonel John E. Phelps, 2 November 1864.

13. *OR*, vol. 13, 201.

Bibliography

Books, Manuscripts, Periodicals.

Alexander, Peter Wellington. Papers. (Microfilm copy of original papers held at Columbia University, NY) University of Arkansas Library, Fayetteville.

Bartels, Carolyn M., trans. *Confederate States Army Trans-Mississippi Order and Letter Book*. Two Trails Publishing, 2000.

Barton, O.S. *Three Years with Quantrill: A True Story Told By His Scout John McCorkle*. 1914. Reprint, Norman: University of Oklahoma Press, 1992.

Bearss, Edwin C. "The Army of the Frontier's First Campaign: The Confederates Win at Newtonia." *Missouri Historical Review* 60, no. 3 (April 1966): 283-319.

Blunt, James G. "General Blunt's Account of His Civil War Experiences." *Kansas Historical Quarterly* 1 (May 1932): 211-265.

Blunt, James G. Letter to Captain Tholen, 7 October 1863, in the Civil War Narratives at the Kansas State Historical Society, Topeka.

Britton, Wiley. *The Civil War on the Border*. 2 vols. New York: G.P. Putnam's Sons, 1899.

Britton, Wiley. *Memoirs of the Rebellion on the Border, 1863*. 1882. Florissant, Mo.: Inland Printer Limited, 1986.

Britton, Wiley. *The Union Indian Brigade in the Civil War*. Ottawa, Kans.: Kansas Heritage Press, 1922.

Brownlee, Richard. *Gray Ghosts of the Confederacy: Guerrilla Warfare in the West, 1861-1865*. Baton Rouge: Louisiana State University Press, 1958.

Buckley, Gail. *American Patriots: The Story of Blacks in the Military from the Revolution to Desert Storm*. New York: Random House, 2001.

Buresh, Lumir F. *October 25th and the Battle of Mine Creek*. Kansas City, Mo.: The Lowell Press, 1977.

Castel, Albert. *A Frontier State at War: Kansas, 1861-1865*. Ithaca (NY): Cornell University Press, 1958.

Castel, Albert. "Kansas Jayhawking Raids into Western Missouri in 1861." *Missouri Historical Review* 54, no. 1 (October 1959): 1-11.

Castel, Albert. *General Sterling Price and the Civil War in the West.* Baton Rouge: Louisiana State University Press, 1968.

Castel, Albert. *William Clarke Quantrill: His Life and Times.* New York: Frederick Fell, Inc., 1962.

Clippings. Baxter Springs Massacre. Baxter Springs Historical Museum.

Confederate Organizations, Officers, and Posts 1861-1865: Missouri Units. Springfield, Mo.: Ozarks Genealogical Society, Inc., 1988.

Connelley, William E. *Quantrill and the Border Wars*, Cedar Rapids, Iowa: The Torch Press, 1910.

Connelley, William E. Papers. Box 13. Kansas State Historical Society.

Connelley, William E. Interview with John Koger. Connelley Collection, Western History Department, Denver Public Library.

Cornish, Dudley T. *The Sable Arm: Black Troops in the Union Army 1861-1865.* 1956. Reprint, Lawrence: University Press of Kansas, 1987.

Cornish, Dudley T. "Baxter Springs Massacre." Unpublished Manuscript in the Johnston Public Library at Baxter Springs, 1963.

Cottrell, Steve. *The Civil War in the Ozarks.* The author, 1984.

Cottrell, Steve. *Effects of the Civil War on the Early Settlers in the Area of Present-Day Joplin.* The author, 1986.

Cutler, William G. *History of the State of Kansas.* Chicago: A. T. Andreas, 1883.

Dugdale, B. I. An unpublished account of the Baxter Springs Massacre in the Civil War Narratives at the Kansas State Historical Society, Topeka.

Edwards, John N. *Shelby and His Men: The War in the West.* Cincinnati: Miami Printing and Publishing Co., 1867.

Fellman, Michael. *Inside War.* New York: Oxford University Press, 1989.

Fryman, Robert J. *"Engaged the Enemy Again": An Assessment of the 1862 and 1864 Civil War Battlefields at Newtonia, Missouri.* Atlanta: Garrow and Associates, Inc., 1995.

Goodrich, Thomas. *Black Flag: Guerrilla Warfare on the Western Border, 1861-1865*. Bloomington: Indiana University Press, 1995.

Gregg, William H. *A Little Dab of History without Embelishment* (sic). Unpublished Manuscript. Western Historical Manuscript Collection, University of Missouri, Columbia.

Hale, Donald R. *We Rode with Quantrill*. Lee's Summit, Mo. The Author, 1982.

History of Cass and Bates Counties, Missouri. St. Joseph, Mo.: National Historical Company, 1883.

History of Greene County, Missouri. 1883. Reprint, Clinton Mo.: The Printery, 1969.

History of Henry and St. Clair Counties, Missouri. 1883. Reprint, Clinton, Mo.: Henry County Historical Society, 1968.

History of Hickory, Polk, Cedar, Dade, and Barton Counties, Missouri. Chicago: Goodspeed Publishing Co., 1889.

History of Newton, Lawrence, Barry, and McDonald Counties, Missouri, pt. 1. Chicago: Goodspeed Publishing Co., 1888.

History of Vernon County, Missouri. 1887. Reprint, Clinton, Mo.: The Printery, 1974.

Hively, Kay. Interview, July 10, 1999.

Hulston, John K. and James W. Goodrich. "John Trousdale Coffee." *Missouri Historical Review* 77, no. 3 (April 1983): 272-295.

Ingenthron, Elmo. *Borderland Rebellion*. Branson., Mo.: The Ozarks Mountaineer, 1980.

Leslie, Edward E. *The Devil Knows How to Ride*. New York: Random House, 1996.

Livingston, Joel T. *A History of Jasper County and Its People*. vol. 1. Chicago: The Lewis Publishing Co., 1912.

"Lydia Stevens Thomas." *The Club Member* 5, no. 2 (May 1907): 4-5.

Monaghan, Jay. *Civil War on the Western Border, 1854-1865*. Boston: Little, Brown, and Co., 1955.

North, F.A. *History of Jasper County, Missouri*. Des Moines: Mills and Co., 1883.

Norton, Richard L., ed. *Behind Enemy Lines: Memoirs and Writings of Brigadier-General Sidney Drake Jackman*. Springfield, Mo.: Oak Hills Publishing, 1997.

O'Flaherty, Daniel. *General Jo Shelby: Undefeated Rebel.* Chapel Hill: The University of North Carolina Press, 1954.

Pearson, William N. *Sherwood: The Forgotten Village.* The author, 1978.

Peterson, Richard C. et. al. *Sterling Price's Lieutenants: A Guide to the Officers and Organization of the Missouri State Guard 1861-1865.* Shawnee Mission, Kansas: Two Trails Publishing, 1995.

Population Schedules of the Seventh and Eighth Censuses of the United States. Washington, D.C., National Archives and Records Service.

Rea, Ralph R. *Sterling Price: The Lee of the West.* Little Rock: Pioneer Press, 1959.

Regimental Letter Book, 1st Kansas Colored Infantry. (Microfilm M858, Roll 5). National Archives and Records Administration—Central Plains Region, Kansas City, Missouri.

Schrantz, Ward L. *Jasper County in the Civil War.* 1923. Reprint, Carthage, Mo.: Carthage Kiwanis Club, 1988.

Shalhope, Robert E. *Sterling Price: Portrait of a Southerner.* Columbia: University of Missouri Press, 1971.

Snead, Thomas L. *The Fight for Missouri.* New York: Charles Scribner's Sons, 1886.

Speer, John. "The Burning of Osceola, Missouri, by Lane, and the Quantrill Massacre Contrasted," *Transactions of the Kansas State Historical Society* 6: 305-312.

Steele, Phillip W. and Steve Cottrell. *Civil War in the Ozarks.* Gretna, La.: Pelican   Publishing Co., 1993.

Supplement to the Official Records of the Union and Confederate Armies. Wilmington, N.C.: Broadfoot Publishing Co., 1994.

Van Gilder, Marvin L. *Jasper County: The First Two Hundred Years.* The Jasper County Commission, 1995.

Violette, Eugene Morrow. *A History of Missouri.* 1918. Reprint, Cape Girardeau, Mo.: Ramfre Press, 1960.

War of the Rebellion: *A Compilation of Official Records of the Union and Confederate Armies.* Washington, D.C.: Government Printing Office, 1880-1902.

Weldon, Steve. Interview. June 29, 1999.

Young, A.J., ed. *History of Dade County and Its People.* The Pioneer Historical Company, 1917.

Newspapers

Baxter Springs News.
Carthage (Mo.) Weekly Press.
Carthage (Mo.) Evening Press.
Columbia Missouri Statesman.
Emporia News.
Fort Scott Democrat.
Fort Scott Union Monitor
Fort Scott Western Volunteer
Girard (Kans.) Press.
Joplin Globe.
Kansas Cosmos.
Kansas City Daily Journal of Commerce.
Kansas City Daily Western Journal of Commerce.
Kansas City Weekly Western Journal of Commerce.
Leavenworth Daily Conservative.
Leavenworth Daily Times.
Leavenworth Weekly Conservative.
National Tribune.
New York Times.
St. Joseph Weekly Herald.
St. Louis Daily Missouri Democrat
St. Louis Daily Union
St. Louis Tri-Weekly Missouri Republican.

Index